THE POCKET BOOK OF

# Dinosaurs

# THE POCKET BOOK OF
# Dinosaurs

## An Illustrated Guide to the
## Dinosaur Kingdom

**DOUGAL DIXON**

Salamander

**A Salamander Book**

The Chrysalis Building
Bramley Road
London W10 6SP
United Kingdom

© Salamander Books Ltd., 2004

An imprint of **Chrysalis** Books Group

All correspondence concerning the content of this volume should be addressed to Salamander Books Ltd.

ISBN 1-84065-555-0

Color reproduction by Anorax Imaging
Printed in Malaysia

# Contents

# Introduction

Oh no! Not another dinosaur book!

But, oh yes. There is always room for a new dinosaur book. There will never be enough books to cover the whole story of dinosaurs. The study of these marvelous beasts was established nearly two hundred years ago, and from the first discoveries of isolated bones in Victorian England the science of vertebrate paleontology spread out across Pioneer North America, uncharted Asia, mysterious Africa, isolated Australia, and frozen Antarctica. With approximately three or four hundred different types of dinosaur discovered and named to date, you would think that we know all there is to know. The truth is that every month, every week, every day even, new discoveries are coming to light that tell us something new about these magnificent beasts. It has been estimated that there may have been something like about 1500 different types, and so we have only found about a fifth of them. They just keep on coming.

Even as I write this introduction the news of the discovery of a new dinosaur from North Africa is hitting the headlines. This discovery does not just present us with a glimpse of a new and fascinating animal in itself—a new genus to add to our three or four hundred—but also tells us something about the time and place where it lived.

During the 160-odd years that constituted the age of the dinosaurs, the landmasses of the world changed considerably. At the beginning all the dry land consisted of a single supercontinent, that we call Pangaea. As the age of dinosaurs got under way this great landmass split up into the individual continents and began to move to the positions that they now occupy. Different dinosaurs then evolved on different continents. This new dinosaur was found in North Africa, but belonged to a dinosaur family that has so far only been known from South America and India. Until now we could visualize these dinosaurs evolving on the southern part of Pangaea that had still not split into the individual continents but was isolated from the continents in the north. Now that this southern dinosaur has been found on a northern continent we are going to have to rethink the geographical evolution of our planet.

It used to be understood that dinosaurs, being reptiles, were cold-blooded. Then, in the wake of newer ideas that perhaps some of them at least were warm-blooded like mammals or birds, came discoveries of dinosaur remains in Australia, in an area that would have been well within the Antarctic Circle when the dinosaurs were alive. And at the same time extensive dinosaur remains appeared in the far north of Alaska. Suddenly dinosaurs were no longer the warm-weather-loving sluggish tropical beasts of yore, now they had the ability to live in all sorts of hostile terrains, under all sorts of harsh climatic conditions. Appreciation of them changed overnight.

The way in which the relation between dinosaurs is defined by shared characteristics, such as the number of bones in the hip, the presence of a certain bone in the jaw, or something truly esoteric, like the density of serrations on a tooth or the angle of curvature of a rib—anything that the paleontologist finds that may be significant. However, there are all sorts of gray areas in this, such as the question of whether or not particular characteristics are relevant and evolved from an ancestor that had them. It is quite possible for the same characteristic to evolve quite independently in totally different animals—the wings on a bat and a bird give a rather good example (they both have wings but evolved at different times and in different ways). That is what makes the science so exciting.

So, it is obvious that the science does not stand still. By the time that you read this book new discoveries will be found and more theories will be produced. It will be impossible to stay abreast of all the discoveries all the time.

In science an animal is known by its scientific name, or its "binomial." For example, people are *Homo sapiens*. Dinosaurs are the only animals that are commonly known by their scientific name, for example, *Tyrannosaurus rex*. The scientific name of an animal consists of its genus name and its species name, people are *Homo* (genus name) *sapiens* (species name). The names are usually derived from Latin or Classical Greek. It is customary usually to use only the genus name for dinosaurs in popular literature. We see *Tyrannosaurus rex* (genus and species names) as simply *Tyrannosaurus* (genus name). In scientific papers once the genus name has been introduced it is often then referred to merely by its genus initial, along with its species name. This has crept into popular literature—how often do we see references to *T. rex?* Note that both genus and species names are always given in *italics,* and that the genus name is capitalized but the species name is not. This should go some way to explaining the usage of names in this book.

To help keep pace with what's happening when and where in the book, as we discuss the dinosaurs, each chapter has a timeline, placing the dinosaurs within their historical period, and a distribution map, showing where the animals in the illustrations were found. There are two ways of doing a distribution map for dinosaurs. We could show a map of the world at the particular period the animals lived and show what part of this ancient geography they inhabited. The other way is to show the modern world and show where their fossilized remains have been found. For this volume we have opted for the latter approach.

Last, but by no means least, it's worth noting that not all animals of the age of dinosaurs were dinosaurs. There was a whole range of other big fascinating reptiles as well. In the sea there were long-necked plesiosaurs, short-necked whale-like pliosaurs, dolphin-shaped ichthyosaurs, big swimming lizards called mosasaurs— no relation to dinosaurs whatsoever. In the skies there were flying reptiles called pterosaurs. These, however, although not dinosaurs themselves, were distantly related to dinosaurs as crocodiles, sharing an ancestor amongst the primitive crocodile-like reptiles known as the thecodonts. However, this distant relation doesn't make pterosaurs any less interesting— ranging from the size of a sparrow to an airplane, their history has also changed, from cumbersome, gliding dinosaurs to nimble and athletic flyers. Hence, these popular and eternally fascinating four-limbed animals with membranous wings appear in the last quarter of the book.

It would require an enormous

volume to discuss dinosaur discoveries, the evolution of theories over time and dinosaur development (and all the dinosaurs that might have existed!), to discuss the bones and muscles and how we think they worked, and much more. This volume is a concise, engaging look at these magnificent beasts and I hope that this sparks an interest for you to go out and discovery more. Meanwhile, get ready to take a step back in time and discover dinosaurs and pterosaurs that will amaze and astound.

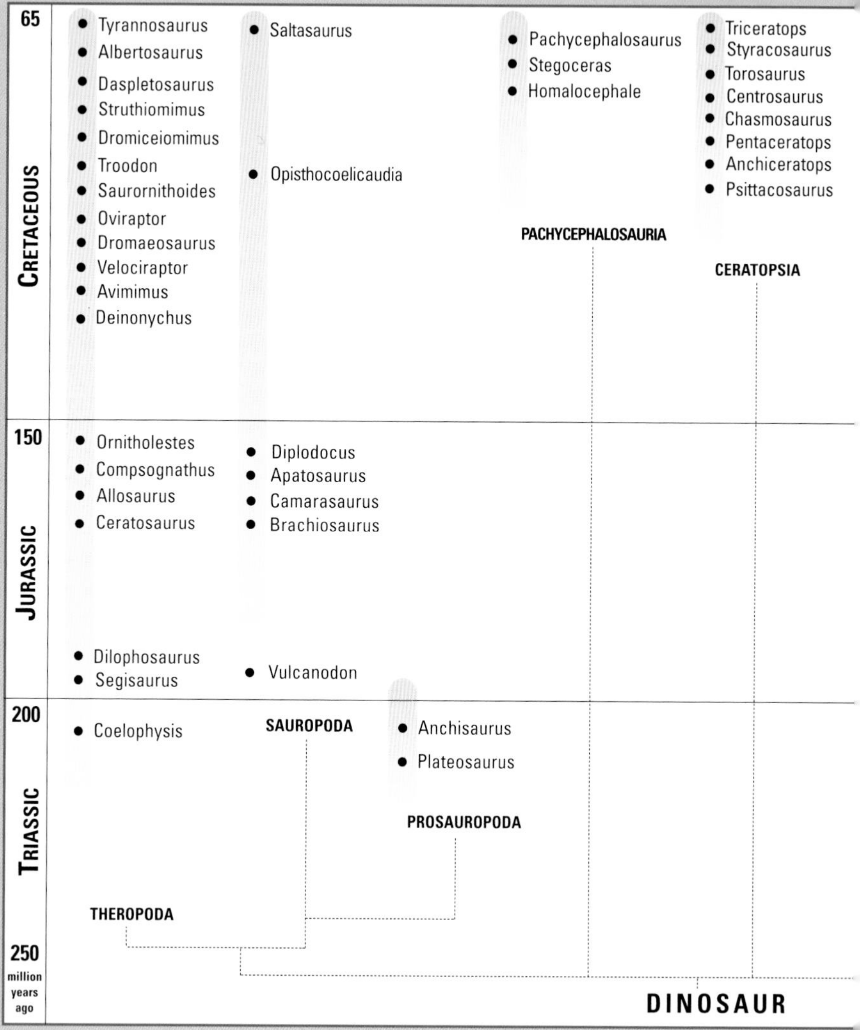

| 65 | | | | |
|---|---|---|---|---|
| | • Tyrannosaurus | • Saltasaurus | | • Triceratops |
| | • Albertosaurus | | • Pachycephalosaurus | • Styracosaurus |
| | • Daspletosaurus | | • Stegoceras | • Torosaurus |
| | • Struthiomimus | | • Homalocephale | • Centrosaurus |
| | • Dromiceiomimus | | | • Chasmosaurus |
| | • Troodon | • Opisthocoelicaudia | | • Pentaceratops |
| | • Saurornithoides | | | • Anchiceratops |
| | • Oviraptor | | | • Psittacosaurus |
| | • Dromaeosaurus | | | |
| | • Velociraptor | | **PACHYCEPHALOSAURIA** | |
| | • Avimimus | | | **CERATOPSIA** |
| | • Deinonychus | | | |

**CRETACEOUS**

| 150 | | | |
|---|---|---|---|
| | • Ornitholestes | • Diplodocus | |
| | • Compsognathus | • Apatosaurus | |
| | • Allosaurus | • Camarasaurus | |
| | • Ceratosaurus | • Brachiosaurus | |

**JURASSIC**

• Dilophosaurus
• Segisaurus          • Vulcanodon

| 200 | | | |
|---|---|---|---|
| | • Coelophysis | **SAUROPODA** | • Anchisaurus |
| | | | • Plateosaurus |

**TRIASSIC**

**PROSAUROPODA**

**THEROPODA**

| 250 |
|---|
| million years ago |

**DINOSAUR**

- Anatotitan
- Edmontosaurus
- Corythosaurus
- Parasaurolophus
- Saurolophus
- Tsintaosaurus
- Tenontosaurus
- Ouranosaurus
- Muttaburrasaurus

- Hypsilophodon
- Iguanodon

- Euoplocephalus
- Pinacosaurus
- Nodosaurus

- Polacanthus

- Hyaelosaurus

**ANKYLOSAURIA**

- Quetzalcoatlus

- Nyctosaurus
- Pteranodon

- Phobetor
- Dsungaripterus
- Pterodaustro

- Gnathosaurus
- Batrachognathus  - Ctenchasma
- Sordes  - Gallodactylus
- Scaphognathus  - Germanodactylus
- Anurognathus  - Pterodactylus
- Rhamphorhynchus

- Dryosaurus
- Camptosaurus

- Stegosaurus
- Kentrosaurus

- Tuojiangosaurus

**STEGOSAURIA**

**PTERODACTYLOIDEA**

- Heterodontosaurus
- Lesothosaurus
- Scutellosaurus

- Scelidosaurus

- Dimorphodon

**ORNITHOPODA**

**THYREOPHORA**

- Preondactylus
- Peteinosaurus
- Eudimorphodon

**RAMPHORHYNCHOIDEA**

# FAMILY TREE

# PTEROSAURS

# Small Theropods I

The most basic type of dinosaur was probably the small theropod. It would have been the first to evolve, and would not have differed much from the thecodonts that preceded it.

The body layout was quite simple, a small crocodile-like body was carried on strong hind legs, held horizontally, and balanced by a heavy tail. The jaws were long and toothy and the head held out at front. A pair of small arms was held clear of the ground, and usually used for grasping.

It was such a successful design that small theropods of this basic shape flourished throughout the age of dinosaurs.

## HAZY ANCESTORS

Immediately prior to the appearance of the dinosaurs, many thecodonts had this same body plan. The Triassic rocks are full of fossil skeletons of lizard-like or crocodile-like animals with long hind legs and heavy tails. Being meat-eaters it was advantageous to be able to run after their prey, and to have the killing teeth and grasping claws held out to the front.

Compsognathus, Coelophysis, *and Ornitholestes* *are quite representative of the small meat-eating dinosaurs that existed throughout the age of dinosaurs. They were all fleet-footed and had a rather bird-like build.*

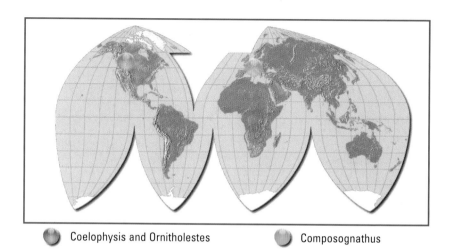

Coelophysis and Ornitholestes        Composognathus

There is a theory that the strong hind legs and heavy tail first evolved as swimming organs in crocodile-like semi-aquatic thecodonts, and that subsequent land animals with these features easily evolved into the two-footed meat-eating dinosaur shape that we know so well.

So what is the difference between an advanced thecodont and a primitive dinosaur? Where does the transition come? We usually define a dinosaur by the arrangement of hipbones, the structure of the anklebone, and the shape of the bones of the skull. Apart from the skull detail these features mostly relate to how a

230        220        210        200        190        180        170        160        15

TRIASSIC                                    JURASSIC

SALTOPUS
COELOPHYSIS

dinosaur walked. Unlike lizards and most modern reptiles, they walked with their legs held vertically with the weight of the body at the top.

The advanced thecodonts would have run lizard-like, although some of them had a tendency toward an upright stance. Many modern lizards can rise up on their hind legs and run for some distance. However, they do not do so like dinosaurs. Their legs cartwheel about at the side in a flailing sprawling gait—not the efficient legs-under-the-body gait of a dinosaur. A running bird like an ostrich would be the modern equivalent of a dinosaur at speed.

Running with a sprawling gait, as a lizard might, would have needed a complex ankle joint to take the stresses. Running with an upright gait would have allowed a much simpler and stronger joint between leg and foot. And it is this simple ankle joint that is one of the defining features of a dinosaur, and it was the strength of such a joint that

## FACTFILE

**The word "theropod" means "beast footed." Victorian scientists seemed to see a resemblance between the foot of a meat-eating dinosaur and that of a mammal, rather than that of a lizard, as in the sauropods, or that of a bird, as in the ornithopods.**

eventually allowed the evolution of big heavy animals.

However, the *Saltopus*, from the Triassic rocks of Scotland is a good example of how problematic it can be to define type; it had long jaws and sharp teeth, short front legs, and a small body. Some paleontologists regard it as a very primitive dinosaur, while others think it is an advanced thecodont. Unfortunately the hipbones are missing from the only known skeleton of *Saltopus* and without those it is impossible to come to a consensus.

| 140 | 130 | 120 | 110 | 100 | 90 | 80 | 70 | 60 |

CRETACEOUS

COMPOSOGNATHUS

## A RANGE OF SMALL TYPES

Small theropods have sometimes been classed together and given the name "coelurosaurs." The definition of the coelurosaurs tends to be rather vague and variable and so we shall dispense with it in this volume. You may, however, come across it in other dinosaur books.

The classification of small dinosaurs is constantly undergoing revision. The difficulty is that dinosaurs, and particularly small dinosaurs, very rarely fossilize. Think of a land animal dropping down dead. What happens to it? It is torn to pieces by scavenging beasts, the meat is consumed, and the bones broken and scattered. Eventually even the hard parts break down and decompose and there is nothing left to fossilize.

Sometimes, though, a land animal falls into a stream or a lake and dies, and may settle on the bottom, if scavenging fish do not eat it. If the water currents do not break up the body, it may be covered in sediment. If the action of groundwater does not rot the remains away it may become fossilized as the sediments turn to

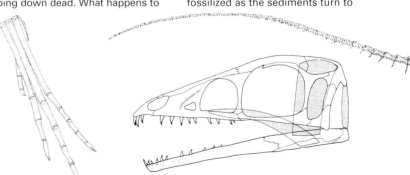

**Above**: *The* Composgnathus *foot was a typical theropod foot. The weight was borne on the three middle toes. The first toe was small and did not reach the ground, and the fifth toe was a rudimentary splinter of bone.*

**Above:***The edges of the gaps in the* Composgnathus *skull held the muscles that opened and closed the jaws. The little teeth were sharp and suitable for catching and eating any small living thing.*

stone. If the resulting sedimentary rock does not remain deep underground it may eventually appear at the surface and begin to erode. If somebody is passing by and notices part of the fossilized skeleton in the rock, there is a chance that an excavation may be mounted to save it before it too turns to dust under the relentless onslaught of the weather. Only if the dinosaur's remains survive every stage of this process are we likely to have a dinosaur fossil to study.

Big, elephant-sized herbivore skeletons are relatively easily found compared with those of delicate chicken-sized carnivores. The fragile bones of these rarely survive. Only under really exceptional circumstances do we find the bones of small theropods, and such circumstances are as likely to preserve an entire skeleton as a single bone. We know of a number of perfect skeletons of small theropods, including those of *Compsognathus* and *Coelophysis*.

Compsognathus *skeleton shows the lightly-built running legs and the typical saurischian pelvis, with all the hip bones radiating away from the socket where the leg was attached.*

# Small Theropods II

The tiny skeleton of *Compsognathus* (see page 17) was one of the first complete dinosaur skeletons to have been discovered, back in 1861. It was found in the same beds as the famous complete skeletons of the first bird *Archaeopteryx*. Even at that time scientists were struck by the similarity between the skeleton of the little dinosaur and that of the first bird. In fact one of the few known skeletons of *Archaeopteryx* languished in a private collection for decades erroneously labeled as a *Compsognathus*. As part of the wider evolutionary debate of the mid-nineteenth century (Darwin's *Origin of the Species* was published in 1859) the theory went around that birds had actually evolved from dinosaurs. It was a theory that was ahead of its time.

*The bird-like appearance of the small theropods is seen in* Segisaurus *(left) and* Avimimus *(right). It is quite likely that at least some of the small meat-eating dinosaurs were covered in feathers.*

## BIRD-LIKE FEATURES

By the turn of the century the dinosaur-bird connection had fallen out of favor. It was not until the 1960s, with the discovery of new bird-like dinosaurs such as *Deinonychus*, that this theory became prominent again. Then, in 1981 *Avimimus* was found. This had the typical small theropod shape, but the upper arm bone

had a shelf, very much like that in the arm bone of a bird—a shelf that in a bird is used to support the wing feathers. The idea was emerging that some small dinosaurs may have been covered in feathers and were related to birds.

*Segisaurus* was a fox-sized theropod, known from only one skeleton discovered in the

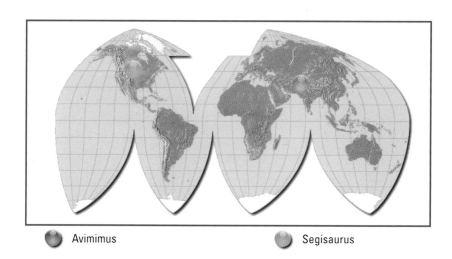

🔵 Avimimus         🔵 Segisaurus

1930s. The remarkable feature of this skeleton was the presence of what seemed to be a fircula, or a wishbone—something thought to have been possessed only by birds. In a bird the fircula is an essential part of the wing mechanism. Since then, however, a fircula has been found in many species of dinosaur, from the agile *Velociraptor* to the mighty *Tyrannosaurus*. (the latter has never been regarded as a flying animal!).

This adds weight to the idea that birds evolved from dinosaurs. A big problem has always been that the dinosaurs that show these

| 230 | 220 | 210 | 200 | 190 | 180 | 170 | 160 | 15 |
|---|---|---|---|---|---|---|---|---|

TRIASSIC                         JURASSIC

▬▬▬ SEGISAURUS

characteristics actually appear later in the geological column than the earliest birds. This makes the sequence of events all wrong—we cannot be the ancestors of our own grandparents. However, an intriguing recent suggestion is that these dinosaurs may have had flying bird-relatives amongst their ancestors, and subsequently lost their powers of flight as did ostriches and emus. They retained the specialist features such as the fircula since those earlier times.

### THE LOST WORLD OF LIAONING

The presence of feathers on certain small theropods was finally proved in the 1980s when a whole suite of fossils came to light in lower Cretaceous lake deposits in Liaoning province in eastern China. *Sinosauropteryx* was a small theropod like *Compsognathus*, but its fossil was so beautifully preserved that it showed a covering of downy feathers. Another discovery, not yet formally named, was of a small *Velociraptor*-like dinosaur with a covering of feathers on the body and face, an almost wing-like structure of feathers on the arms, and a broad fan of feathers at the tip of its long tail.

Together with these discoveries, all sorts of animals, such as *Caudipteryx*, *Microraptor*, and *Protarchaeopteryx* were found, which all seemed to combine dinosaur features with bird features. True birds were found here

## FACTFILE

The only drawback to the dinosaur-bird connection is the hands. Both dinosaur and bird hands are composed of three fingers reduced from the ancestral five. However the three in the dinosaur hand are digits 1, 2, and 3, while those in a bird hand are 2, 3, and 4. There is still a need for a satisfactory explanation.

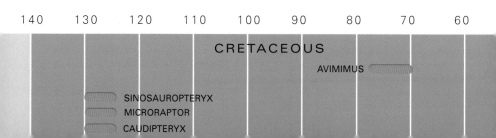

| 140 | 130 | 120 | 110 | 100 | 90 | 80 | 70 | 60 |

CRETACEOUS

AVIMIMUS

SINOSAUROPTERYX
MICRORAPTOR
CAUDIPTERYX

as well, many sporting primitive body parts such as toothy jaws and clawed fingers on the wings, indicating that the transition between dinosaurs and birds was not a straightforward evolutionary step.

## ACTIVE LIFESTYLE

One of the most important interpretations of these animals is the conclusion that these were not cold-blooded lizard-like reptiles, but warm-blooded creatures like birds.

For decades there has been a debate on this subject. The traditional view was that dinosaurs, in common with all other reptiles, were cold-blooded. This does not mean that their blood was actually cold. It is a shorthand term meaning that there was no internal mechanism for regulating the temperature of the body. When the weather was warm, they were warm and active. When the weather was cold, they became cold and sluggish. They were capable of lots of strenuous activity, but these bursts of energy were separated by long periods of rest and recuperation.

However, if the dinosaurs were warm blooded, they would have been able to regulate their own body temperature, allowing them to be active whatever the temperature of their surroundings. Such a mechanism keeps mammals and birds active all the time. A feature of a warm-blooded animal is the presence of an insulating covering— hair or feathers. Only animals that generate their own body heat need to be insulated in this way.

The implications are immense. A warm-blooded animal needs to consume about ten times as much food as a cold-blooded animal of the same size. This means that they would spend most of their time in a hunt for food. They were active all

the day long.

All in all there are around a hundred similarities between small theropods and birds. These include three-toed feet, similar ankle and wrist joints, hollow bones and, as we now know from some of them, feathers.

In fact, the similarities are so strong that many scientists cannot regard birds as a group of their own. In some books, traditional dinosaurs are referred to as "non-avian dinosaurs" to distinguish them from what we would regard as birds.

Taxonomic purists feel they must regard modern birds as nothing but very advanced dinosaurs. So the dinosaurs did not become extinct—they just grew wings and flew away!

**Top**: *The arm bone of* Avimimus *has a bony crest along the rear side. Modern birds have this for the attachment of feathers. Possibly this served the same function in* Avimimus.

**Left**: *This skeleton of* Segisaurus *shows that it was evidently small and agile with short arms and powerful grasping hands. The lack of head hides any clues as to diet and relationships with other early theropods.*

# Medium-Sized Theropods

The early evolution of the dinosaurs from their thecodont ancestors was largely based on a specialization of the leg bones, to allow them to run more efficiently. Nowhere was this development taken to a more logical extreme than in the evolution of the so-called ostrich mimics. We mentioned earlier that a running ostrich is the most apt modern equivalent to a running dinosaur. Towards the end of the Cretaceous period there was a group of theropods that were built remarkably like modern running birds.

## OSTRICH MIMICS

*Struthiomimus* is the best known of the ostrich mimics. It had a tiny head, a long flexible neck, a short body, and very long legs. So far, so ostrich-like. However, it also had big hands with three long clawed fingers and a long stiff tail to balance.

It is a fact that the more advanced, or "derived" in scientific parlance, an animal becomes the more it diverges from the general appearance of the group. We have defined the theropods as having, amongst other things, long toothy jaws. The ostrich mimics

Dromiceiomimus *(back) and* Struthiomimus *(front) belonged to the group of theropods we call the "ostrich mimics." Although they may have looked like ostriches,* Oviraptor *(center) were probably more closely related to birds than the others were.*

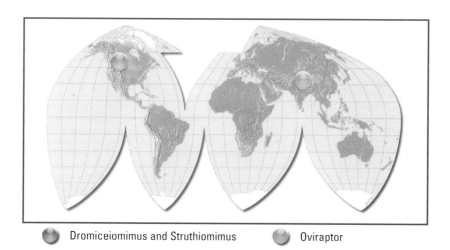

Dromiceiomimus and Struthiomimus        Oviraptor

depart from this pattern by having no teeth in the jaws at all. In fact, the best specimens of the skull show a kind of a fluted pattern to the edges of the jaw. This was once interpreted as a sieve-like structure used for filtering plankton from inland lakes, as flamingos do. It now seems more likely that this pattern showed the site of attachment of a horny beak—a practical substitute for teeth.

So, where did the teeth go? There have been two schools of thought; first, that over evolutionary time the teeth became fewer and fewer until they disappeared altogether, and second,

230      220      210      200      190      180      170      160      15(

TRIASSIC                                    JURASSIC

that the teeth became finer and finer, diminishing in size until they ceased to exist. The second theory gained some weight in the 1980s with the discovery of a primitive ostrich mimic in Spain, called *Pelecanimimus*. It had quite long jaws with tiny little teeth, far more teeth than would be expected in such a dinosaur. It also had what appeared to be a pouch of skin beneath the jaw like that of a pelican—hence its name.

## THE OSTRICH MIMIC DYNASTY

There were several different types of ostrich mimic, and they were all very similar to one another. One rather startling find, though, is of a pair of arms that were about 8 feet (2.4 meters) long. They seem to have come from an ostrich mimic, but if they did their owner must have been almost *Tyrannosaurus* size. The name given to this mysterious beast is *Deinocheirus*— "terrible hands."

The fact that *Struthiomimus* and the

other ostrich mimics had beaks suggests that they departed from the main image of a theropod in another way—instead of eating meat they ate plants. Since we usually define the theropods as being the meat-eating dinosaurs this poses something of an anomaly. Digesting plant material needs a much bigger volume of intestine than digesting meat, and there does not seem to be enough room for a plant-eating digestive system in the body of *Struthiomimus*. Perhaps they ate only highly nutritious plant material like fruit, or perhaps they ate insects as well. This is an area that is being actively investigated by paleontologists.

Another recent discovery is significant. We have seen that some, perhaps all, of the small theropods were warm-blooded. The covering of feathers is one of the main areas of evidence. Evidence for this appears in the ostrich mimics too. A particularly

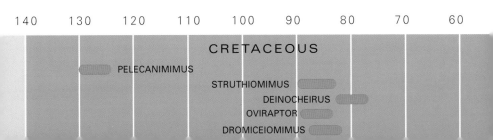

140    130    120    110    100    90    80    70    60

CRETACEOUS

PELECANIMIMUS

STRUTHIOMIMUS

DEINOCHEIRUS

OVIRAPTOR

DROMICEIOMIMUS

good specimen found in Canada in the 1990s shows unmistakable marks on the arm bones—marks that indicate the attachment of wing-type feathers. So perhaps the ostrich mimics too were warm-blooded and covered in feathers. Like today's ostrich they may have had plumes on their forelimbs for display. This would all make sense. A long-legged running animal that obviously had an active lifestyle would very likely have been warm-blooded.

## EGG THIEF?

In the 1920s there was a famous series of expeditions mounted by the American Museum of Natural history, under the leadership of a flamboyant paleontologist called Roy Chapman Andrews. The first of these expeditions headed into the Gobi desert of Mongolia with the aim of finding traces of early man. Instead they found dinosaurs.

The most important find of the trip was the discovery of dinosaur nests and eggs. Until that time it had been assumed that dinosaurs had laid eggs, but there had never been any proof available. The Gobi expeditions found many skeletons of the primitive horned dinosaur *Protoceratops*, at

different stages of growth. These were so prolific that later paleontologists have dubbed them "the sheep of the Cretaceous." Also in the area, there were nests full of eggs. They had stumbled upon the dinosaurs' nesting site.

By one of the nests lay the skeleton

of an odd-looking theropod. It had long hands and a strange short face. There were no teeth in the powerful jaws, just a pair on the roof of the mouth. This theropod was dubbed *Oviraptor*, "egg-thief," and it had evidently been killed in the act of robbing a *Protoceratops* nest.

*Oviraptor* seemed ideally adapted as an egg-thief. The long clawed hands could have grasped the egg, and the powerful jaw could have crushed through the shell, assisted by the pair of teeth in the roof of the mouth. And this was accepted wisdom for seventy years.

Then, in the 1990s another

**Below:** *The neck of* Struthiomimus *was quite mobile, but the back and the tail were quite rigid. The broad ilium bone at the top of the hips held the powerful running muscles.* Struthiomimus *had long foot bones that were light and slender. The toes were worked by tendons from muscles further up the leg. This gave a lightweight foot that could be moved quickly—ideal for running.*

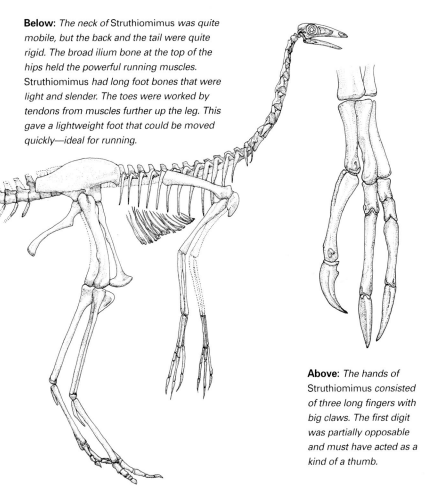

**Above:** *The hands of* Struthiomimus *consisted of three long fingers with big claws. The first digit was partially opposable and must have acted as a kind of a thumb.*

American expedition to the Gobi found another well-preserved skeleton of *Oviraptor*. This time it was not caught in the act of robbing a nest, it was actually sitting on the nest incubating the eggs. The "egg-thief" had not been an egg thief at all—the nests had been *Oviraptor* nests all the time.

The fossil of the *Oviraptor* on the nest is extremely elegant. Its legs are folded beneath it and the arms are spread out over the egg clutch. The eggs were arranged in concentric rings, partly buried in the sand. If the arms were feathered this would have provided an insulating blanket for the eggs.

## A RANGE OF OVIRAPTORS

Since the discovery of the first *Oviraptor* in the 1920s several other closely related types have been found, all with characteristic short jaws. Most had crests on their heads, a bit like those of the modern cassowary, and probably used for display. Some had long tails, like other theropods, while others had short, stumpy tails with fused bones at the end.

The short tail with the fused bones suggests an anchor for big feathers. Modern birds have such a structure supporting their tails. This, along with the evidence for feathered arms spread over incubating eggs points to

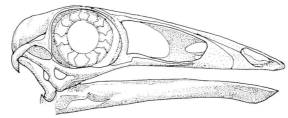

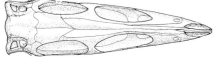

**Above, left and right** : *Although the theropods were the meat-eating dinosaurs, it is possible that the ostrich mimics may have been omnivorous, supplementing their carnivorous diet with shoots and fruits.*

**Above**: *We do not know what* Oviraptor *ate. The jaws were short and furnished with a powerful beak (to the left, the eye socket is the roundish hole in the middle), and the only teeth were a pair on the roof of the mouth. Perhaps it crushed eggs or shellfish.*

the likelihood that *Oviraptor* and its relatives were feathered as well.

Other features of the anatomy have suggested to some contemporary paleontologists that *Oviraptor* should actually be classed as a bird and not a dinosaur (or rather a "non-avian dinosaur").

So, if these animals were not egg-stealers, what was the purpose of the very strange jaw and teeth arrangement? We are still not sure of that one. Nuts and mollusks have been suggested as the main foodstuff, but the mouth still looks like a very efficient egg-crushing device.

# Maniraptorans

Since its discovery in 1905, and for decades onward, the image of *Tyrannosaurus* strode the pages of paleontological literature secure in its reputation as the fiercest hunting animal that ever lived—the king of the tyrant lizards. But, in 1964 a whole new group of dinosaurs began to come to light, and these challenged the king's position.

Imagine a tiger-sized dinosaur, with sharp teeth and huge grasping hands armed with sharp talons. Equip it with a killing claw on the hind foot, as big as the fang of a saber-toothed cat, and articulated so that it could swing round in a scything action—designed for disemboweling huge prey. Then postulate that this was, in fact, a warm-blooded animal, and intelligent enough to unite in packs to bring down whatever quarry it chose. You are imagining *Deinonychus*—"terrible claw."

## THE JAWS THAT BITE; THE CLAWS THAT SNATCH

It would be easy to say that almost overnight the scientific perception of a typical dinosaur as a slow-moving, sluggish, dim-witted, dragon-like monster changed with this discovery.

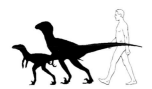

However as in all disciplines it takes a long time for established ideas to change. It was the discovery of *Deinonychus* that alerted the scientific community that the dinosaurs may actually have been warm-blooded. It was *Deinonychus* that had the very bird-like skeleton that pointed to the evolutionary connection between the dinosaurs and the birds. There were, however, so many entrenched arguments to the contrary that the debate raged for decades. The killing claw was particularly interesting. A complex joint kept it clear of the ground and free from damage while it was not being used.

*The maniraptorans, including* Velociraptor *(left),* Deinonychus *(center), and* Dromaeosaurus *(right), were perhaps the most bird-like of the dinosaurs. Such active animals must have had a warm-blooded metabolism and were probably covered in feathers.*

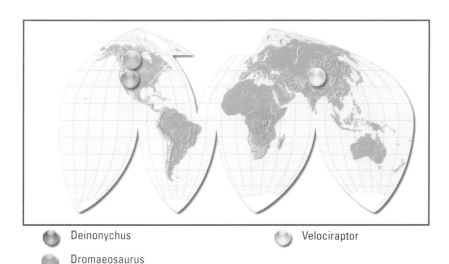

🌓 Deinonychus           🌕 Velociraptor

🌑 Dromaeosaurus

It was not unlike the claw of a cat, which could be raised out of the way when it was not actually being used for killing. Another feature was the wrist joint. Early restorations show the fingers curled downward. It is now believed that at rest the hands were held with the palms facing inwards—the better for grasping prey with. When not being used the arms were held up against the chest, folded away like the wings of a bird.

One thing was very clear, though. These features defined a whole new group of dinosaurs—a group that we now call the maniraptorans— the "hunters with hands."

**Right**: Deinonychus *seemed to have hunted in packs. There is at least one fossil occurrence of the remains of several* Deinonychus *that have feasted on a big plant-eater (in this case Tenontosaurus—see p.106). However* Deinonychus *was so fast that it could have easily run down the small fleet-footed plant-eaters like Hypsilophodon (see page 106) while hunting on is own.*

## PLENTY OF RAPTORS

The first of the group to have been discovered was fox-sized *Dromaeosaurus*, back in 1914. Only the head and part of the foot were known, and so it was a long time before the true nature of the animal was clear. The shape of the rest of the body is inferred by comparison with others of the group. It actually appeared quite late in the history of these animals, in the late Cretaceous period, but, it was quite primitive. The slashing claw was fairly small and the skull was quite heavy compared with its relatives. Perhaps it still relied on its teeth for doing most of its killing.

Another early discovery was of wolf-sized *Velociraptor*. This was found in Mongolia during one of the American Museum of Natural History expeditions of the 1920s. There again it was a long time before we had a really good idea of what the whole animal was like. This came in 1972 with the discovery of a complete *Velociraptor* skeleton wrapped around the skeleton of a *Protoceratops*. It had grabbed the head of the horned dinosaur and its killing claw was deep into its body. But the *Protoceratops* had fought back—its beak was clamped around the meat-eater's forearm. Neither won the fight, however. A sandstorm buried both and they were fossilized together.

Although the maniraptorans were generally fairly small and lightweight animals, there have been a few discoveries that suggest that there were very large representatives of the group. *Utahraptor* is known only from a handful of bones found in late Cretaceous rocks of Utah. These include the core of what was probably a 14-inch (35-centimeter) long killing claw. The entire animal must have been about 21 feet (6.5 meters) long, but, for all that there are exhibits in several

| 230 | 220 | 210 | 200 | 190 | 180 | 170 | 160 | 15 |
|-----|-----|-----|-----|-----|-----|-----|-----|-----|

TRIASSIC

JURASSIC

museums, the mounted skeletons that are sometimes on show are largely conjectural. The other giant is Argentinean *Megaraptor*. We only have the claw and bits, but if it were a maniraptoran it would have been even bigger than *Utahraptor*.

## STAR BILLING

It may have been a long time before science accepted the significance of the maniraptorans, but the public caught on quickly. In the 1994 film "Jurassic

**Above**: *The skeleton of Deinonychus is unusual in that the hip bones were arranged like those of a bird, with the pubis bone swept back. This pattern evolved dependently several time in the dinosaurs—here, in the maniraptorans, in the ornithischians, and also in the birds themselves.*

| 140 | 130 | 120 | 110 | 100 | 90 | 80 | 70 | 60 |
|---|---|---|---|---|---|---|---|---|

## CRETACEOUS

DEINONYCHUS

DROMAEOSAURUS

THERIZINOSAURUS

VELOCIRAPTOR

BEIPAIOSAURUS

MEGARAPTOR

UTAHRAPTOR

TROODON

MONONYKUS

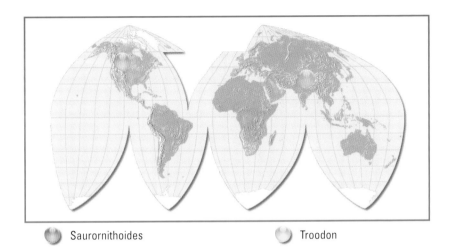

Saurornithoides        Troodon

Park," *Velociraptors* were the bad guys. At the time much was made of the fact that the *Velociraptors* in the film were too big—the size of tigers rather than of wolves—and enlarged for dramatic effect. In fact, the animals portrayed were not *Velociraptor* at all, but *Deinonychus*. At the time there were several conflicting ideas about the classification of the maniraptorans, and one version maintained that *Deinonychus* was a species of *Velociraptor*. It was this version that the film adopted.

It is interesting to note that, even in the entertainment media, ideas tend to develop slowly. The maniraptorans in "Jurassic Park" had leathery naked skin, no feathers. Those in the 1998 ground-breaking BBC series "Walking With Dinosaurs" were likewise reptile-skinned. Nowadays when a maniraptoran is shown it is usually shown feathered, for example, Discovery Channel's "Dinosaur Worlds, White Tip's Journey" in 2003. Perhaps this also traces the evolution of the computer generated image technology that allows for the detailing of feathered bodies that could not be shown ten years previously.

## MANIRAPTORAN MISCELLANY

The maniraptoran classification extends to a broad group of animals. One particular group consists of the troodonts, including *Troodon* itself.

These were more lightly-built than *Velociraptor* and *Deinonychus*, approaching the proportions of the ostrich-mimics, and the killing claws were smaller. The head was much smaller in proportion to the body and the eyes were quite large. The eye

**Above:** *Troodonts, such as the* Saurornithoides *(left) and* Troodon *(right), combined the agility of ostrich mimics with the killing apparatus of the maniraptorans.* Troodon *(right) was probably the most intelligent dinosaur that we know, but that only give it the brain power of some of our more primitive birds.*

sockets show that the eyes were directed to the front. This indicates that they had binocular vision, useful for

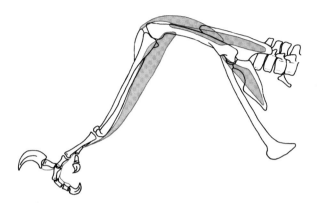

**Left**: Deinonychus's *main weapon of attack would have been the leg with its huge claw, rather than the jaws and teeth of a typical predator.*

judging distances and very valuable for a hunting lifestyle. It has been suggested that the large eyes showed that these animals hunted at night.

A peculiar feature of the skull was the size of the brain. For the size of the animal, it was the biggest brain of all dinosaurs, approaching the relative size of the brain of some of today's birds. This may sound impressive, but the birds with the comparable brain size are the emus and cassowaries—intellectual lightweights of the bird world. The intellegence of the maniraptorans had been greatly exaggerated.

Another group of maniraptorans

consists of the alvarezsaurids. The first of these, *Mononykus*, was found in the Gobi desert. When it was found no-one quite knew what to make of it. The arms were short and thick and had a huge single claw each—they were almost like stubby wings. This was hardly the hunter with hands that was implied by the term maniraptoran. The first thought that occurred was that this was actually a kind of flightless bird, and in fact once a life restoration was done with the animal covered in feathers it did look very much like a bird. But what of the big claw?

Theories abound, including the idea that it was used for digging, or for

**Left**: *The foot and claw of* Deinonychus: *It has four toes, the first, spur-like, the second with an enormous claw, and the other two were used for running.*

ripping open termite mounds. The alvarezsaurids ranged in size from chicken-sized to turkey-sized animals.

So what do we make of the therizinosaurs, or, as sometimes termed, the segnosaurs They consist of a peculiar group of animals that seem to fall into no obvious category.

*Therizinosaurus* itself is typical. It had a small head, toothed more like a plant-eating prosauropod than a meat-eating theropod. It had a long neck and a dumpy body, but the remarkable feature was its hands. It had scythe-like claws, each one as long as a man's arm. They could have been used for gathering plant material, or even for digging into termite mounds. The therizinosaurs seem to have been covered in downy feathers—a specimen called *Beipaiosaurus*, from the same lake deposits in Liaoning, in China, that provided the excellent fossils of the half-bird half-dinosaur beasts, shows the therizinosaur's

downy covering quite well. These diverse features make the therizinosaurs almost impossible to classify. However, certain features of the skull suggest that they may be descended from a branch of the maniraptoran family, and that is why they are included here.

And lastly, in the grand scheme of things, it may be that the birds themselves must be classed as maniraptorans too, since they seem to have been descended from the early members of this group.

# FACTFILE

A maniraptoran was as nimble as a ballerina. Balanced by a tail that was stiffened with bony tendons, rigid as a pole, it could stand on one foot and slash with the claw of the other.

# The Bigger Theropods

The big boys were the ones with the jaws and claws—the big meat-eating dinosaurs. They were once classified as "carnosaurs" in the same way as the smaller theropods were classified as "coelurosaurs," but they cover such a wide range of animals that they cannot really be lumped together. Nowadays we sometimes come across the term "carnosauria" with a definition referring only to the group of theropods to which *Allosaurus* and its closest relatives belong—such is the confusing nature of dinosaur taxonomy.

As we have seen, the mammal-like stance of the dinosaur, with vertical legs, allowed the development of a heavy body. The earliest theropods were quite small but they soon developed into monsters.

### LOOKING AT ALLOSAURUS

Perhaps *Allosaurus* was the most typical of the big meat-eating dinosaurs. It was quite common in late Jurassic North America. At 30 feet (9 meters) long it was the biggest meat-eater of the time and place. An even bigger specimen is known—about 39 feet (12 meters) long—and some paleontologists regard this as a species of *Allosaurus* but others think it a totally different animal altogether and call it *Saurophaganax*.

In common with the rest of the theropod group *Allosaurus* had long jaws and sharp teeth. Its skull

*Big meat-eating dinosaurs such as* Allosaurus *(left) and* Ceratosaurus *(right) had powerful hind limbs and powerful jaws. Most had heavy claws on their hands as well, to catch and hold their prey.*

was made up of the
usual lightweight arrangement
of struts and flanges, loosely knitted
together. As well as giving strength this
also provided some flexibility. The bones of the
skull could bow outward while eating, to allow the
animal to swallow huge chunks of flesh. The thickest
parts of the skull were the bones that formed the jaws.
Deep inside these we find a series of growing teeth, all fitting
inside one another like cones. When one tooth broke off or

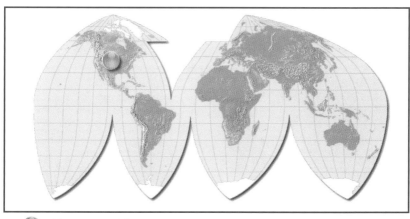

Allosaurus and Ceratosaurus

dropped out—a common occurrence in view of the violent lifestyle—there was always another one growing to take its place. This gave rise to an irregular "snaggle-toothed" appearance to the tooth row. The top of the skull carried bumps and knobs that, in life, probably formed the base of an arrangement of small horns or crests. This massive head was supported on a short but flexible neck. It was habitually carried in a typical S-shape.

The body was deep but not very long, and the arms were short. Short they may have been, but they would have been very strong. The hand was three-

230    220    210    200    190    180    170    160    15

TRIASSIC                JURASSIC

DILOPHOSAURUS

fingered, the first having the biggest claw and the third being rather small.

The hip bones were the typical lizard-like shape that was shared by all theropods. The three hip bones radiated away from the hole that held the leg joint. At the top was the plate-like ilium that held the leg muscles. Sweeping down toward the back was the ischium. The third bone was the pubis and this reached down and forward and ended in a broad "boot." When the dinosaur lay down on its stomach, the pubis bone took the weight of the hip region. All these bones were paired, and the two pubis bones were joined along their length with only a gap at the top. The intestines were carried in front of this pair of bones, with the large intestine passing through the gap and out towards the rear.

The leg bones, as we have seen, were held vertically. The ball, of the ball-and-socket hip joint, stuck out of the side at the top of the femur and fitted into the gap in the hip bones. A small shelf of bone in the hip just above the gap stopped the ball from popping out.

Judging by the way the leg bones were articulated it seems as if the knee joint was permanently flexed, while the lower leg and foot bones were in a line, with a straight ankle joint.

The feet were typically digitigrade, that is, the animal walked on its toes. Toes two, three, and four contacted with the ground, while toe one was small and pointed backward and toe five was hardly there at all. The spread of the three main toes provided a broad surface area that took the weight of the animal.

The tail was broad and heavy. Its function was to balance the forequarters. In life its hunting tools—its teeth, and clawed hands—would have been held out at the front where they would have been the most use.

| 140 | 130 | 120 | 110 | 100 | 90 | 80 | 70 | 60 |
|---|---|---|---|---|---|---|---|---|

CRETACEOUS

ALLOSAURUS
CERATOSAURUS
YANGCHANOSAURUS

## THE KILLER

Proof that this was a powerful killing machine comes in the form of tooth marks on bones belonging to the plant-eating sauropods of the time. These tooth marks match exactly the shape, size, and arrangement of the teeth in the jaws of an *Allosaurus*. What's more, broken *Allosaurus* teeth are found lying around the dismembered skeletons of these big plant-eaters. This points to the violence involved in tearing away at the massive corpse. Loss of the odd tooth would not have been a tragedy—we have already seen that the jaws of an *Allosaurus* were adequately equipped with growing spares.

An interesting sideline on the life of *Allosaurus* comes in the form of recently discovered footprints. One set, from Utah, shows where the *Allosaurus* was lying on the ground with the weight of its forequarters supported by its forearms. Another set from Canada shows gouges made by three-clawed fingers by the side of a track of foot-prints. We can visualize an *Allosaurus* perhaps lying in wait for its prey, and then making its charge from a sprinter's start.

## NEIGHBORS

*Allosaurus* was not the only big meat-eating dinosaur around in late Jurassic North America. *Ceratosaurus*, from a distance, would have looked like a smaller version. Its main difference was its ornamentation. Its head was furnished with an array of horns, with a particularly big one on the nose, and there was a ridge of scutes down the backbone, producing a serrated crest like that seen in depictions of dragons.

The fact that more than one type of big meat eater lived in the same time and place means that they must have had different lifestyles. Perhaps they hunted different food and chased different dinosaurs. Perhaps they followed one

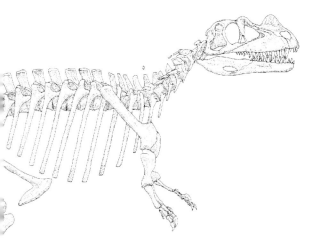

**Left**: *The skeleton of* Ceratosaurus *is of a typical big meat-eating dinosaur. The body is held horizontally, balanced at the hips by the tail, so that the killing teeth of the jaws are held well forward.*

another around, and when, say, the *Allosaurus* made a kill, the *Ceratosaurus* or a pack of *Ceratosaurus* would close in and wait for the hunter to eat its fill and then finish off the remains.

So many "perhapses" here. It will be a long time before we can say that we know everything about dinosaur times.

### An Early Meat-Eater

The big meat-eaters were not restricted to the late Jurassic. Nor were they restricted to North America. They evolved over and over again throughout the age of dinosaurs and on all continents.

An early one was *Dilophosaurus*. This was much more lightly-built than *Allosaurus* and had a pair of semi-circular crests on its head. It also had a prehensile arrangement of bones at the front of the mouth. This gave the mouth a rather odd look, but it probably meant that it could manipulate small struggling food. It could have spent its time winkling lizards out of crannies or little mammals from holes in tree trunks. Certainly the thin crests would suggest that it did not tackle big prey that would have put up a fight. All shapes of meat-eaters. All shapes of food.

**Ceratosaurus Skull dorsal and front View**

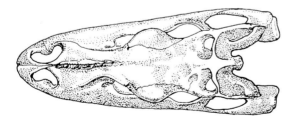
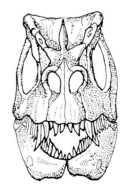

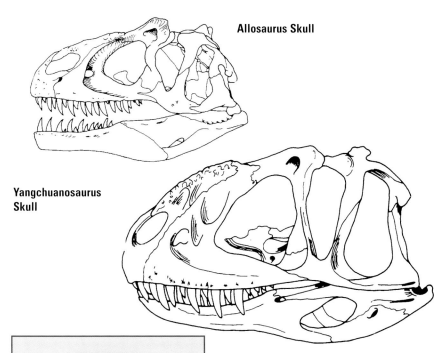

**Allosaurus Skull**

**Yangchuanosaurus Skull**

## FACTFILE

The very first dinosaur to be discovered was one of the big meat-eaters. In 1824 Dean William Buckland, then Reader in Geology at Oxford University, studied a fossil jawbone set with vicious teeth. He saw that it was the jawbone of a big reptile and named it *Megalosaurus* or "big reptile."

**Left and above**: *The body plan of the big meat-eaters tended to be very similar, but their heads differed.* Ceratosaurus *had a horn on the nose.* Dilophosaurus *(see title page) had a pair of bony crests on the head.* Allosaurus *had a skull that was very light-weight for the size.* Yangchanosaurus *was very similar to* Allosaurus, *showing that similar animals lived in North America and China.*

# Tyrannosaurus

*T*yrannosaurus, Tyrannosaurus rex, T.rex . . . The name itself is redolent of power, evocative of giant ferocity. For a century this has been the beast that exemplified dinosaur power at its greatest. It has been the icon of mindless strength for generations. The story of its discovery is no less wonderful.

### THE DISCOVERY

On the desk of William Hornaday, the director of the New York Zoological Society, lay a piece of fossilized bone as a paperweight. One day in 1902 it was noticed by the famous fossil hunter Barnum Brown, who recognized it for what it was—a piece of the horn of a *Triceratops*. Intrigued, Brown began to trace the history of the piece. Looking at photographs of the area in Montana where Hornaday had picked up his trophy while hunting, Brown recognized the land-scape as good dinosaur country and organized an expedition.

Travel in the United States was not so easy in those days. Brown took a train to Miles City in Montana, and then a five-day wagon trek to the town of Jordan—the nearest settlement to the site of the find. He was now in the midst of the badlands, formed of the eroded and jagged outcrops of the appropriately named Hell Creek formation of the upper Cretaceous. As soon as he pitched camp he saw a skeleton in the ground, easily recognized by the chocolate brown

*The tyrannosaurs were the biggest meat-eaters of the northern continent at the very end of the age of dinosaurs. They included* Tyrannosaurus *(right),* Albertosaurus, *and* Daspletosaurus, *all from North America, but others existed in Asia.*

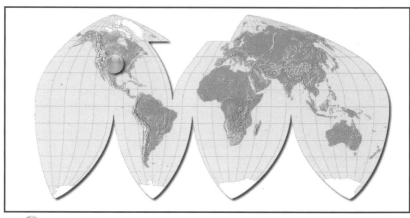

Tyrannosaurus rex

color of the fossilized bones against the blue of the hard sandstone. He could see straight away, even in the fading light, that this was the skeleton of something completely new.

Exciting though this was, Brown left it until he could tackle it properly, and turned to some more easily excavated skeletons nearby. It was three years later that he returned to this skeleton with a full excavation team, and the new beast was transported to New York in crates.

Henry Fairfield Osborn, director of paleontology at the American Museum of Natural History identified

| 230 | 220 | 210 | 200 | 190 | 180 | 170 | 160 | 15 |
|---|---|---|---|---|---|---|---|---|
| TRIASSIC | | | | | JURASSIC | | | |

it as a meat-eating animal, far bigger than anything so far discovered. He gave it the genus name *Tyrannosaurus*, meaning "tyrant lizard" and the species name *rex*, meaning king. So, the king of the tyrant lizards was revealed to science in 1905. No Hollywood producer could have invented a star name that was so in keeping with the part it would play in the minds of everybody, scientist and public alike, for the next century.

This original specimen was incomplete, and so Brown went to hunt for a better one. The man's luck was in, for he discovered a far more complete *Tyrannosaurus* skeleton in 1907. It took three years for his team to excavate it and return it to New York. This is the skeleton that is currently mounted in the American Museum of Natural History.

At first the mounted skeleton was partially conjectural. The front limbs were missing, and they were reconstructed with three fingers rather than the two we now know it possessed. Many of the tailbones had been lost, and the mounted skeleton showed a tail that was far too long. The biggest error, however, was in the stance. It was mounted with its back at forty-five degrees and the tail dragging, kangaroo-like, on the ground. This was the image of *Tyrannosaurus* that was, from then onward, in the public mind. A redesigning of the dinosaur halls in the museum in the 1990s involved the remounting of the *Tyrannosaurus* skeleton in its proper pose and its proper dimensions.

## TYRANNOSAUR SCANDAL

Since Brown's original discovery there have been about twenty *Tyrannosaurus* skeletons found. This is quite a large number, most dinosaurs are known from a single specimen, and an incomplete one at that.

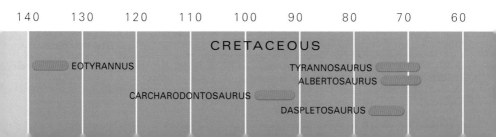

| 140 | 130 | 120 | 110 | 100 | 90 | 80 | 70 | 60 |

CRETACEOUS

EOTYRANNUS

TYRANNOSAURUS

ALBERTOSAURUS

CARCHARODONTOSAURUS

DASPLETOSAURUS

Perhaps the most famous and the most complete is that of the *Tyrannosaurus* affectionately dubbed "Sue." It was spotted in the ground in the badlands of South Dakota by Susan Hendrickson while out hiking in 1990. She reported it to a local fossil research organization, the Black Hills Institute. The researchers there, Peter and Neal Larsen, obtained permission from the landowner and excavated it, bringing it back to the Institute for study. Then the trouble started. The Sioux Nation claimed that they owned the land and that the skeleton was extracted without their permission. The federal government then decided that the skeleton was their property and none of them—Black Hills Institute, original landowner, Sioux Nation—had any right to it. In an armed dawn raid in 1992 mounted by the FBI, the National Guard, and US Marshals the skeleton was confiscated. It lay decaying under armed guard in a government cellar for months until the matter was cleared up. The settlement involved Peter Larsen going to jail and the fossil being put up for auction. Chicago's Field Museum finally obtained it, putting in a bid for eight million dollars, and it is now on display in the main atrium there.

## TYRANNOSAURUS LIFE

With all these skeletons available you would think that we would know all about *Tyrannosaurus* and how it lived. It was a meat-eater, certainly, the teeth tell us so. It ate big dinosaurs. We know this because unmistakable teeth marks have been found in the bones of *Triceratops*, and fragments of hadrosaur bones have been found in tyrannosaur droppings. Here, scientific opinions diverge.

The classic image of *Tyrannosaurus* is of a huge hunter, dodging the horns of defensive *Triceratops* while it lunges at the vulnerable body behind the neck shield, or bursting out of cover, mouth open, and bearing down on a herd of duckbills too scared to move. However, there is a body of evidence that suggests that *Tyrannosaurus* was not an active hunter at all, but a slow-moving scavenger,

lumbering around the late Cretaceous landscape sniffing out and finding the decaying carcasses of animals killed by more agile predators.

## FACTFILE

*Tyrannosaurus* was not the only tyrannosaur. The other main tyrannosaur was the smaller and earlier *Albertosaurus*. Others, such as big-toothed *Daspletosaurus* and the Asian *Tarbosaurus*, are regarded by some scientists as merely different species of *Tyrannosaurus* rather than distinct genera in themselves.

The arguments for a scavenging lifestyle include the animal's enormous size. A weight of over 7 tons does not suggest the build of an active hunter. The articulation at the hips seems to suggest an ability to take only slow short strides. And those tiny arms would be no good in a fight.

**Left**: *The skeleton of* Tyrannosaurus *had to support an active animal weighing up to 7.7 tons. The hips were very strong, to support the great weight, and the skull was quite lightweight.*

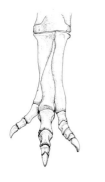 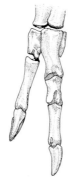

**Left:** *Like its cousin, the* Tyrannosaurus, *the front of the* Tarbosaurus *leg is very small and ends in a feeble, two-fingered hand (far left) which may have been used as a grappling hook. The broad foot (right) indicates three forwardly-pointing toes that end in sharp curved claws.*

On the other hand, the arguments for an active hunting lifestyle include the arrangement of the teeth. Those at the front of the mouth are short and sturdy, designed for holding fast into struggling prey. The eyes point forward to some extent, giving binocular vision and an appreciation of distance—useful for a hunting animal.

Or perhaps it led a combination of lifestyles, hunting big prey when it was ecessary, and scavenging corpses when available.

## RIVALS

For about a century *Tyrannosaurus* was the biggest meat-eating dinosaur known, but its position has now been challenged.

*Giganotosaurus* was discovered in Argentina in 1995, and has a skull that is bigger than any *Tyrannosaurus* skull known. At about the same time new remains were found of a relative of *Giganotosaurus* in North Africa. Originally discovered

**Right:** *If* Tyrannosaurus *was an active hunter rather than a scavenger, it may have hunted by ambush, lying in wait for its prey. When an unsuspecting hadrosaurid came close, the meat-eater would have charged at it with a short burst of speed, crashing into it with jaws agape. The skull was heavily reinforced and would have absorbed the shock of the collision*

in 1931, the known bones of *Carcharodontosaurus* were all destroyed as collateral damage during World War II. The new remains proved this to be an animal as big as, or bigger than *Tyrannosaurus*. *Giganotosaurus* and *Carcharodontosaurus* were both related to the earlier *Allosaurus*, and for now hold the record of the biggest meat-eating dinosaurs known.

## FACTFILE

The earliest tyrannosaur known is early Cretaceous *Eotyrannus* from the Isle of Wight. This was quite small and lightly built. It must have looked like an ostrich mimic with a big head.

# Anchisaurus

The theropods, as we have seen, all belonged to one of the two major groups of dinosaurs—those that had hipbones arranged like those of a lizard. This group is known as the saurischia. The other dinosaurs that belonged to this saurischian group were the heavy, long-necked dinosaurs known as the sauropodomorphs. And these were all plant eaters.

The most primitive of the sauropodomorphs were the prosauropods.

**Below:** Anchisaurus *was a typical small prosauropod. It had a small head on a long neck, and a deep body. It may have been able to move about on two legs or on all fours.*

## SMALL PROSAUROPOD

You could almost imagine a primitive sauropodomorph evolving from a primitive theropod. Just change the diet to plants and everything else is logical.

A diet of plants needs a much more complex digestive system than a diet of meat. Consequently a plant-eater needs a much bigger and deeper body than a comparable-sized meat-eater, just to hold that bigger digestive system. Compare the body of an antelope with that of a cheetah. In a saurischian dinosaur that big digestive system has to be carried well forward of the hips— the paired pubis bones would not allow it to be positioned any further back. This brings the center of gravity forward and the animal has to take up a four-footed stance, no longer able to balance on hind legs. The four-footed

stance implies slightly less mobility and so a long neck develops as an answer to the requirement to reach enough food. Here you have a prosauropod. This is, of course, rather simplistic. The forefoot of a prosauropod retains the ancestral five toes, not the reduced three or two fingers as found on a theropod. A feature of the forefoot of a prosauropod is the presence of a very big first finger (a thumb) carrying a massive claw.

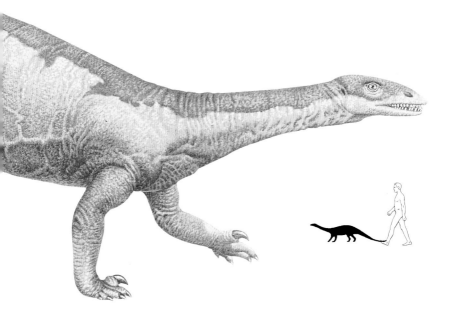

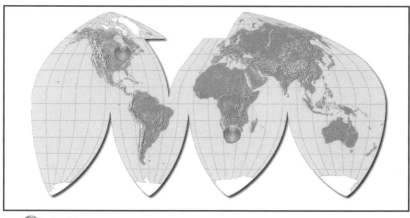

 Anchisaurus

The head, also, is totally different. Instead of the jagged row of sharp teeth, constantly being replaced, we find a fairly even row of teeth that are all about the same size. Whereas the teeth of a meat-eater are often finely serrated like a steak knife, the teeth of a plant-eater may be coarsely serrated like a vegetable grater. The teeth are packed together more closely than in a theropod, and they are angled so that they slightly overlap one another. In the most primitive of the prosauropods, like *Anchisaurus*, the jaw hinge is slightly below the line of the teeth. The musculature implied by this would give a

| 230 | 220 | 210 | 200 | 190 | 180 | 170 | 160 | 15◖ |
|---|---|---|---|---|---|---|---|---|

TRIASSIC          JURASSIC

ANCHISAURUS

THECONDONTOSAURUS

greater leverage to the jaw than in the theropods—an adaptation to tearing off tougher food material.

## ACTIVE PLANT-EATERS

The smaller prosauropods such as *Anchisaurus*, and the even smaller rabbit-sized *Thecondontosaurus*, were not much heavier than equivalent-sized theropods. They must have been able to spend some time on their hind legs.

*Anchisaurus* was one of the first dinosaurs to be discovered in North America, back in 1865, but it was not properly described until 1886 when the pioneer American paleontologist Othniel Charles Marsh studied it. It was also thought to have been one of the earliest plant-eating dinosaurs. This idea was supported by the primitive nature of its skeleton. The rocks in Connecticut in which it was found were regarded as being of the Triassic age. However, in the 1970s they were redated as coming from the early Jurassic, so, although

*Anchisaurus* was a very primitive prosauropod it actually appeared quite late in the history of the group.

Small prosauropods lived all over the world. There are different genera found abundantly in North America, in South America, in Europe, in China, and in southern Africa. At the time the prosauropods lived—Triassic and early Jurassic times—all the landmasses of the world comprised a single supercontinent called Pangaea. Although the center of this supercontinent was so far from the sea that the landscape was one of unbearable desert, the fringes, however, were habitable. Because there were no separate continents the same types of animal lived everywhere. This began to change later in the Jurassic period when the Pangaea began to crack and separate into individual continents. The oldest-known prosauropods lived in what is now Africa. It seems likely that this where they evolved and they later spread to all parts of Pangaea.

| 140 | 130 | 120 | 110 | 100 | 90 | 80 | 70 | 60 |

CRETACEOUS

## FOOTPRINTS

Footprints of dinosaurs are fairly common. However, it is almost impossible to match the footprint to the animal that made it. Unless we find the fossil of the animal itself at the end of a set of tracks there is no way in which a footprint-maker can be identified with certainty. This has occasionally been done in the case of marine invertebrates—it has not so far been successful in dinosaurs. For this reason, scientists give formal scientific names to different types of footprint that do not imply that they are made by one particular animal. The name for this is an "ichnogenus."

One of the few examples of a set of footprints that can be reliably attributed to a dinosaur involves a prosauropod. A fairly common ichnogenus of fossil footprint found in the Lower Jurassic Navajo sandstone in Arizona is called *Navahopus*

*falcipollex*. It is the print of a four-footed animal, with hind feet bigger than the front. The first digit of the front foot shows the mark of a large outward-curving claw. This is so obviously the arrangement of the prosauropod that there cannot be any doubt. The most common prosauropod of that size in that horizon in that region is *Ammosaurus*, and so it seems very likely that the *Navahopus* footprints were made by this animal.

---

# FACTFILE

**In most of the small prosauropods the eye sockets were big while the nostrils were small. This indicates that sight was much more important to these animals than the sense of smell.**

---

**Right:** *With its long flexible neck.* Anchisaurus *would have been able to browse from the branches of trees. It was one of the earliest plant-eating prosauropod dinosaurs.*

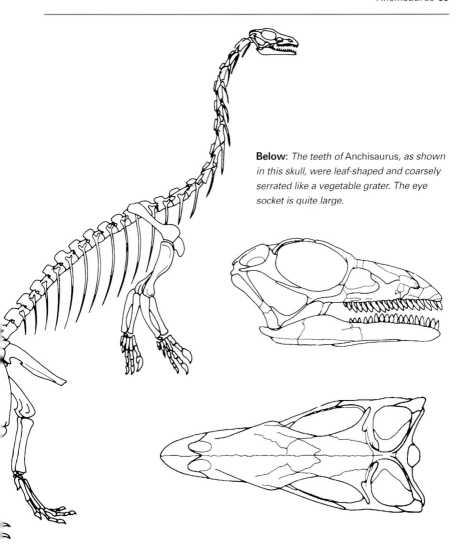

**Below:** *The teeth of* Anchisaurus, *as shown in this skull, were leaf-shaped and coarsely serrated like a vegetable grater. The eye socket is quite large.*

# Plateosaurus

The earliest, and most primitive, prosauropods were quite small—no bigger than the size of a man—but they soon evolved into the giants of their day. One of the biggest of these early plant-eaters was the 26 feet (8 meter) long *Plateosaurus*.

*Plateosaurus* remains have been found in large numbers in Upper Triassic rocks in over fifty places in Germany, Switzerland and France. On the face of it, it looks as if these beasts roamed the Triassic plains of northern Europe in significant herds. An alternative hypothesis is that these were solitary animals that lived on the surrounding hills rather than on the plains themselves. When they died they may have been washed down to the plains individually by mountain streams and rivers, and their bodies gathered together where the currents slackened.

Interestingly, the arrival of the big prosauropods seemed to coincide with the evolution of the sword-leaved coniferous trees, like the monkey puzzles. We could be looking at the results of a Mesozoic arms race here. As the browsing dinosaurs developed, and were able to feed from high in the trees, the trees began to evolve defense mechanisms to protect themselves from them. One such defense would be

**Right:** Plateosaurus *was one of the largest of the prosauropods. When it went on four legs it resembled the massive sauropods that were to follow it.*

the tough blade-like leaves that we see in the primitive conifers.

## NIBBLED AWAY

A fairly common occurrence of fossilized *Plateosaurus* is of limb bones standing vertically in a bed of sandstone. This is a very unusual form of fossilization. Usually when an animal dies, and becomes buried, it lies parallel to the surface, becoming fossilized lying horizontally between the beds of the subsequent rock.

When these vertical limb bones are found, there are usually few remains of the rest of the skeleton—perhaps just a few bones scattered here and there. What are often found, though, are the teeth of meat eaters in the close vicinity. These are the teeth of small theropods, although precisely which theropod cannot be

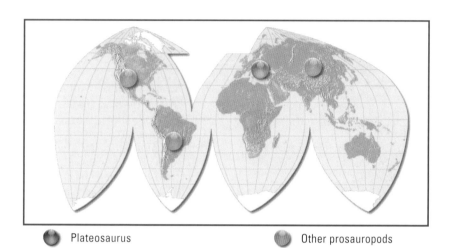

 Plateosaurus           Other prosauropods

ascertained, and the teeth of fierce crocodile-like semi-aquatic reptiles called phytosaurs. A bit of geological detective work can give us an idea of what happened here.

A heavy *Plateosaurus* lumbers down to the bank of a river, possibly to drink. It steps on a sandbank and immediately begins to sink, not realizing that the sandbanks hereabouts are treacherous quicksands. It sinks up to its body in the sand and becomes trapped. Its struggle alerts the meat-eaters of the area and they begin to circle. The phytosaurs attack from the water while the theropods attack from the land. Being

| 230 | 220 | 210 | 200 | 190 | 180 | 170 | 160 | 15 |

TRIASSIC                    JURASSIC

PLATEOSAURUS
MUSSAURUS
MELANOROSAURUS

AMMOSAURUS

lighter animals they are not trapped by the sand. The *Plateosaurus* is helpless and it is soon killed. The hunters tear their victim apart and carry away the pieces, except for the legs that are still buried in the quicksand, and it is these that are fossilized, still in their vertical position.

Prosauropods in South Africa have been found fossilized in similar circumstances.

## PROSAUROPOD POT-POURRI

An interesting anecdote of extended dinosaur discovery is the case of the prosauropod *Ammosaurus*. It was another prosauropod from the Lower Jurassic sandstones of Connecticut, studied by Othniel Charles Marsh. In 1889 Marsh was called to the quarry where the skeleton was found. Unfortunately he was only able to save the rear half, as the front part was encased in a block that had already been cut out by the quarrymen and sold as building material. It was incorporated into a nearby bridge in South Manchester, Connecticut. And there it remained until 1969 when the bridge was demolished and replaced with a more modern structure. The two pieces of *Ammosaurus* were then, after eighty years, reunited.

Consider *Mussaurus*, the "mouse lizard." This prosauropod was first known from a tiny complete skeleton, small enough to lie in the palm of a man's hand. It was discovered in late Triassic rocks in Argentina in 1979. Immediately it was hailed as the smallest dinosaur that ever lived, and slipped into public mythology as such. The remains of four other tiny *Mussaurus* were then found at the site along with some broken eggshell. These remains turned out to be those of tiny hatchlings. The adult *Mussaurus*, though it was never found, has been estimated to have been about 10 feet (3 meters) long—

| 140 | 130 | 120 | 110 | 100 | 90 | 80 | 70 | 60 |

CRETACEOUS

not a really big prosauropod, but certainly not the smallest dinosaur that ever lived. However, even today, we see it hailed as such in books that ought to know better.

Many prosauropod skeletons are known from the Lower Jurassic of China. These include a tiny animal, not much bigger than *Mussaurus*, and given the name *Fulengia*. Another, slightly larger prosauropod from the same area, was named *Tawasaurus*. An even larger one was described and called *Gyposaurus*. Eventually it was decided that these three dinosaurs actually represented the hatchling, juvenile and sub adult stages of the *Plateosaurus*-sized *Lefengosaurus*, known in abundance from that area since the 1940s. Such are the pitfalls in naming new dinosaurs.

## SOME BIGGIES

Some of the prosauropods became really large animals. *Melanorosaurus* and its relatives grew up to about 39 feet (12 meters) in length. They were completely quadrupedal, their great weight disqualifying them from any movement on two legs. Their huge limbs were supported by long, solid bones.

*Melanorosaurus,* with its tiny head, its long neck, and its massive body, could almost be regarded as a primitive sauropod, but certain aspects of the leg bones show that, big as it was, it was still one of the prosauropods. Certainly in appearance and in lifestyle it anticipated the massive sauropods to come.

**Below:** Plateosaurus *skull and tooth*

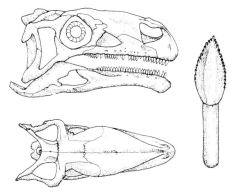

**Below:** *As in all prosauropods,* Plateosaurus *had a five-fingered hand. The first finger had a huge thumb claw, but otherwise it seems to have been a hand for supporting weight. The* Plateosaurus *foot had four big toes and a rudimentary fifth one. The animal could either have walked on tiptoe like a bird or with the whole foot on the ground like a bear.*

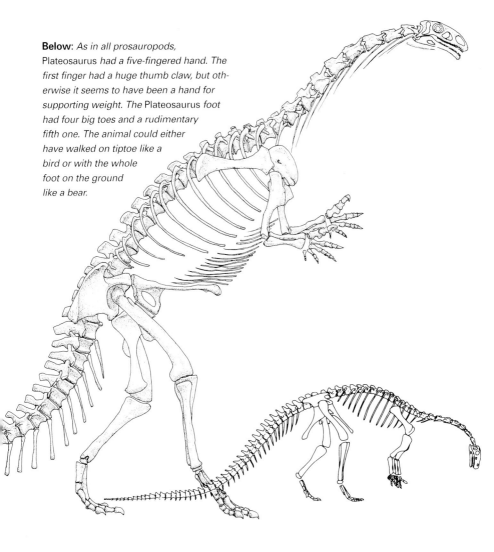

# Vulcanodon

The sauropods were the mighty plant-eaters of the Mesozoic. They were the ones with the elephantine bodies and legs, the long necks with tiny heads, and the long whip-like tails. Their appearance was so distinctive that anyone, with only the slightest grounding in paleontology, could have been able to recognize one from its appearance alone. However, the distinction between advanced prosauropods and primitive sauropods is one of those tricky places where we have only vague evidence and where experts disagree.

The big four-footed *Vulcanodon* discovered in the lower Jurassic rocks of Zimbabwe in 1972 is the most primitive of the sauropods. Or is it? Could it not be an advanced prosauropod, like *Melanorosaurus*? Currently the scientific feeling is that it is actually a primitive sauropod but so distinctive that it merits a family of its own.

Its sauropod features include the strong limb bones, a long forearm, advanced structure of the backbone, flattened hoof-like claws, and a big sharp claw on the thumb. However, this last feature is seen on all prosauropods too. The primitive features are in the details of the hipbones, which seem to be very similar to those of a prosauropod.

Vulcanodon *was one of the most primitive of sauropods. In appearance it looked like something between the prosauropods and the sauropods that were to follow.*

## A PUZZLE

Unfortunately we do not have a complete skeleton available to use for further detection work. The most serious lack is the neck and head. Those shown on the restoration here are entirely conjectural.

The only known skeleton was found with carnivore-like teeth scattered around it. This led to the postulation that it was a carnivorous animal. This theory would have been in keeping with an early view of prosauropod lifestyle.

Because the most primitive of the prosauropods were so close to their meat-eating ancestors people believed that the prosauropods were omnivorous, eating either meat or plants, whatever came their way. This was an idea that prevailed until that latter part of the twentieth century, when more and more work was done on the known prosauropod skeletons, particularly the skulls and teeth. This work showed that they could not have been meat-eaters at all. The carnivore-type teeth that were found with the *Vulcanodon* skeleton must have come from its killer, or some animal that scavenged its corpse after its death.

In South Africa there are a number of dinosaur trackways attributed to the

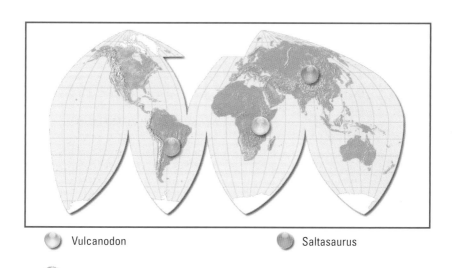

🔵 Vulcanodon        🔵 Saltasaurus

🔵 Opisthocoelicaudia

ichnospecies *Deuterosauropodopus*. (When you see the suffix *–opus* in a scientific name you can be pretty sure you are dealing with an ichnospecies.) The shapes of these footprints are very much like the shape of the feet of *Vulcanodon*, so it seems likely that they were made by this animal.

## INDIAN COUSIN

Another bothersome beast is *Barapasaurus*, from the Lower Jurassic

| 230 | 220 | 210 | 200 | 190 | 180 | 170 | 160 | 15 |
|-----|-----|-----|-----|-----|-----|-----|-----|-----|

TRIASSIC           JURASSIC

OHMDENOSAURUS

VULCUNODON 🔵

ZIZHONGOSAURUS

BARAPASAURUS 🔵

CETIOSAU

GONGXIANOSAURUS 🔵

KOTASAURUS 🔵

ISANOSAURUS 🔵

beds of India. This is known from about half a dozen specimens, but none of these possesses the skull either. What we have here is a very big animal, up to about 59 feet (18 meters) long. The smallest specimen is of an animal about half that size, and it seems that they moved about in family groups with all ages present. Like *Vulcanodon* it had a collection of very primitive prosauropod-like features, and some advanced features that suggest that it was a sauropod. Sauropod vertebrae were evolved to cut down weight but maintain their strength. The vertebrae of *Barapasaurus* had hollows in the side, suggesting an evolutionary stage in the development of lightweight backbones. Again, the main skeleton was confusingly surrounded by meat-eaters' teeth.

*Kotasaurus* is another primitive Indian sauropod with prosauropod features. This time the teeth are known, and they are spoon-shaped, very much like some of the later sauropods.

In early Jurassic times India was still part of the supercontinent of Pangaea, and so it is not surprising that the animals here were similar to those of Africa.

## ALL OVER THE WORLD

*Gongxianosaurus* and *Zizhongosaurus*, found in China, were also primitive sauropods from this time. *Isanosaurus* comes from Thailand and is probably the earliest known sauropod, but it is difficult to fix the time precisely. A leg bone of yet another, called *Ohmdenosaurus*, is known from Germany. This shows how widespread the sauropod group was this early in its evolution.

The very first sauropod to be discovered was *Cetiosaurus*, and this was in England back in 1948. The first bones were thought, by the most eminent anatomist of the day Sir Richard Owen, to have been of aquatic whale-like animals—hence the name,

140　　130　　120　　110　　100　　90　　80　　70　　60

CRETACEOUS

which means "whale lizard." Even when an almost complete skeleton was uncovered shortly afterward, and its true dinosaurian nature revealed, there was a reluctance to abandon the aquatic idea. In fact the idea that sauropods liked water never really went away. For most of the history of paleontology it was assumed that the sauropods were so heavy that they would not have been able to support themselves on land. It was widely believed that they needed to wade about in rivers or swamps so that the water would buoy up their weight.

The long neck and the tiny head would have made an ideal snorkel, allowing the animal to breathe while completely submerged. The vertebrae full of hollows was obviously a buoyancy measure. Anyway, they were so defenseless that they would have needed to surround themselves with water just to keep

**Right**: *The skeleton of* Vulcanodon *is quite heavily built. Later sauropods had finely-sculptured bones with hollows in them to keep down the weight.*

the big meat-eaters away. Water-weeds seemed the most suitable diet for what were believed to have been very weak teeth. Indeed the evidence for an aquatic life for the sauropods seemed over-whelming.

This theory was not dispelled until the 1970s when the true nature of the strong limbs of these magnificent beasts came to light.

**FACTFILE**

The word, sauropod, means "lizard-footed." The arrangement of the bones in the foot were lizard like, as opposed to mammal like in the theropods, and bird-like in the ornithopods.

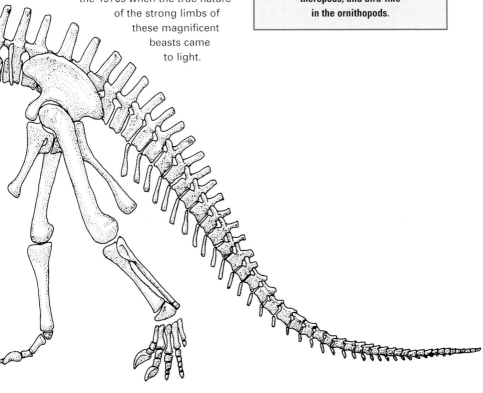

# Diplodocids

If it is length that you appreciate in your dinosaurs then it is the diplodocid group of the sauropods for you.

In this group we find the mighty *Seismosaurus*, from the late Jurassic of New Mexico. When this was found in 1991 it was estimated to have been about 150 feet (45 meters) long. More recent estimates put the length at about 110–120 feet (33–37 meters).

Then there is *Supersaurus*. This is only known from backbones but these suggest that the neck was something like 44 feet (13.5 meters). This would make for a very long animal, but the structure of the rest of the backbone suggests a body that was proportionally small and gives us a total length of 130 feet (40 meters).

We can make these estimates because we know of one member of the group that has been found as a complete skeleton. We use this example to make the comparisons. This dinosaur is *Diplodocus*.

*The diplodocids were the very long, low sauropods. With long necks and whip-like tails,* Diplodocus *(left) and* Apatosaurus *(right) were the best-known, reaching lengths of about 88 feet (27 meters).*

## A PROUD DISCOVERY

The shape of a sauropod is familiar to anybody remotely acquainted with dinosaurs. They are the big plant-eaters with the four legs, the elephantine bodies, the tiny heads, the long necks, and the long tails. Within that pattern there are a number of variations, seen in the different families of sauropods. The diplodocids were the sauropods that went for length.

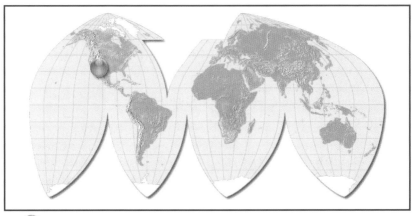

Apatosaurus and Diplodocus

The first remains of *Diplodocus* were found in 1877, but these consisted only of the vertebrae. The main discovery was made in 1902 when dinosaur collector Earl Douglass mounted an expedition to Utah under the sponsorship of steel millionaire Andrew Carnegie. There he discovered an almost complete skeleton of *Diplodocus* and transported it back to the Carnegie museum in Pittsburgh, where it was put on display. It was duly given the species name *Diplodocus carnegii* in honor of its sponsor. Carnegie was so pleased with his dinosaur he ordered replicas to be

| 230 | 220 | 210 | 200 | 190 | 180 | 170 | 160 | 15 |
|---|---|---|---|---|---|---|---|---|
| TRIASSIC | | | | JURASSIC | | | | |

made of the whole skeleton and sent them to museums around the world. The museum director commissioned Serafini Augustini, a local sculptor who specialized in religious medallions, to make molds from the three hundred or so bones in the skeleton and produce permanent casts of them. Ten replica skeletons were produced and they were sent as gifts to the British Museum (Natural History)—now the Natural History Museum in London— and museums in Paris, Frankfurt, Bologna, Berlin, Vienna, and La Plata. As a result, the skeleton of *Diplodocus* has been seen by more people around the world than any other dinosaur.

The skeleton was almost complete. All that was missing were the front feet. Unfortunately, instead of making comparisons with other dinosaurs of the same group, which would be the practice nowadays, they merely put casts of the hind feet on the front for the sake of the mounted skeleton. As a result, for many years *Diplodocus* was depicted with three big claws on its front feet, just like its hind feet, rather than the single claw that we now know it to have had.

## DIMENSIONS

*Diplodocus* reached a length of 88 feet (27 meters). Of this over half was tail. The body itself was about 13 feet (4 meters) long and the rest was neck. The head was very small, about the size of that of a horse, and contained a brain that was no bigger than that of a domestic cat; not much for controlling a body of that length.

The body was light, compared with that of other sauropods, and it was quite nicely balanced in the hip regions. This suggests that *Diplodocus* and the other members of the group could raise itself on its hind legs quite easily to reach food that was high up in the trees. This would make sense as recent research suggests that the

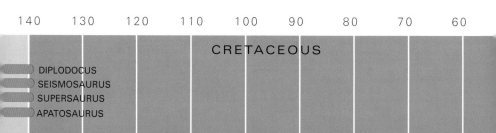

140        130        120        110        100        90        80        70        60

CRETACEOUS

DIPLODOCUS
SEISMOSAURUS
SUPERSAURUS
APATOSAURUS

articulation of the neck-bones would preclude the animal from raising its neck very high from the horizontal.

The tail was long and narrowed to a whip-like point. The shape suggests that it was indeed used as a whip. It could have been used to lash out at attacking theropods, or even for making cracking noises to scare them away, or to alert the rest of the herd.

All of the above is reasonably well known. However, there are other things that are more speculative. In the 1980s,

a discovery in Utah seemed to suggest that *Diplodocus*, or one of its relatives, had spines down its back. The same discovery suggested that, rather than being covered in elephant-like leathery skin as usually depicted, it was covered in overlapping scales like a fish.

## DIGESTION

*Diplodocus* was a plant-eater. Its teeth were pencil-shaped and arranged like the teeth of a rake. Wear on these teeth shows that it could have fed both from

**Right:** *The neck of* Diplodocus *was supported by an extremely strong ligament along the top. This continued down the tail, and the two, anchored on the long spines on the vertebrae of the body, held each other in balance. The lizard-like hips of the sauropods were similar to those of the meat-eating theropods, with the bones radiating away from the hip socket.*

overhanging branches and from undergrowth. There was no mechanism for chewing the food, indeed, it would not have had time to chew its food. To feed that big body it would have had to spend its entire life just raking leaves from the trees and swallowing. What is coming to light now is the likelihood that *Diplodocus* and the other sauropods swallowed stones to help the digestion. Modern plant-eating birds do this. They swallow pieces of grit, and these gather in an area of the stomach called the gizzard and grind up the plant material as it comes down. Discoveries of piles of polished stones associated with sauropod skeletons suggest that the sauropods had gizzards and swallowed stones to help their digestion. Small heaps of polished stones found in beds laid down in sauropod regions suggest that once these stones had worn smooth they were regurgitated and fresh ones swallowed.

Judging by the volume of food required for such a big animal, it seems unlikely that the sauropods were warm-blooded like the small theropods.

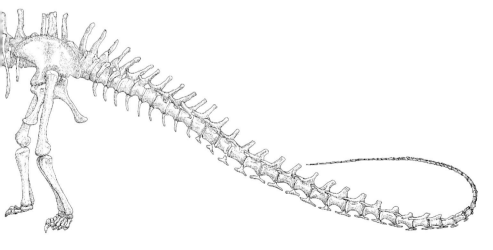

## THE SHIFTING FORTUNES OF APATOSAURUS

The other famous member of the diplodocid family is *Apatosaurus*, which is shorter than *Diplodocus* but much heavier, and lived in the same place and time.

This used to be known by the far more evocative name *Brontosaurus*. In 1877 Othniel Charles Marsh studied the hipbones of a large dinosaur that had just been discovered and named the beast *Apatosaurus*. In 1879 he studied a much more complete skeleton from the same area, which he named *Brontosaurus*. The difference between the two lay in the number of vertebrae fused to the hipbone (sacrum).

In 1903 paleontologist Elmer Riggs was looking at another skeleton of the same dinosaur and realized that both *Apatosaurus* and *Brontosaurus* were the same animal. Dinosaurs added vertebrae to the sacrum as they got older and one of Marsh's originals was a youngster, without its full compliment. So, here we have the same animal but it has been given two names. When a situation like this crops up there is a principle that is always invoked—the first name given is the valid one. However, *Brontosaurus* had crept into public consciousness and it was decades before the valid name *Apatosaurus* became widely accepted.

Another cause of confusion was the head. (*Apatosaurus* was never a lucky animal.) The skeleton found in 1879 was one of the most complete dinosaur

**Below:** *The foot (bottom) and hand (top) of* Diplodocus *were broad and weight-bearing, rather like the feet of an elephant.*

skeletons known, but it, as usual, lacked the head. When reconstructing the skeleton at the American Museum of Natural History in New York a skull was borrowed from another sauropod, *Camarasaurus*, to complete it. *Camarasaurus* lived in the same time and same place as *Apatosaurus*, but was quite a different animal, and the head was much shorter and box-like. In the early 1900s the true skull of *Apatosaurus* was identified—it was long and low, very much like that of *Diplodocus*—but, despite that, the wrong skull was attached to the *Apatosaurus* skeleton until the 1970s.

**Left and below**:
Diplodocus *had a skull that was long and low. The teeth were arranged like those of a rake, for combing leaves from trees.*

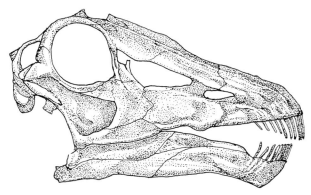

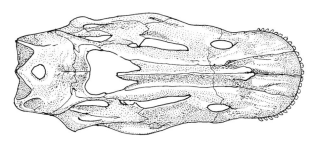

# Camarasaurids and Brachiosaurids

If the diplodocids went for length then the brachiosaurids went for height.

The first specimen of *Brachiosaurus* was found in Colorado by Elmer Riggs in 1900. It lay in the Morrison Formation—a vast sweep of late Jurassic sandstones and mudstones that stretch from New Mexico to Canada, laid down in a broad arid plain crossed by forest-banked rivers and dotted with seasonal lakes. It was the Morrison Formation (named after a town that is now effectively a suburb of Denver, at the foot of the Rocky Mountains) that provided the skeletons of the diplodocids and of many other dinosaurs that typify Jurassic North America.

The animal became really famous in 1909, when an expedition from the Berlin Museum unearthed a whole dinosaur graveyard in the Jurassic rocks of what is now Tanzania. As in the early days of fossil excavation in North America, the African expedition was arduous. From the port of Dar es Salaam it took two days to travel by steamboat to the closest port of the site.

*Brachiosaurids and camarasaurids, such as Brachiosaurus (left) and Camarasaurus (right), were the sauropods that went for height rather than length. Their necks towered 39 feet (12 meters) above the ground, reaching into the tops of trees.*

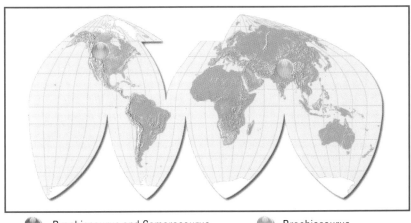

🌐 Brachiosaurus and Camarasaurus  🌐 Brachiosaurus

This was followed by a four-day trek inland to reach the small village of Tendaguru where the fossils were found. All equipment was carried by porters. In four years of excavation over 250 tons of fossil material was shipped back to Germany. The prize of this collection was an entire *Brachio-saurus* skeleton. When mounted in the Humboldt Museum in Berlin this massive beast stood 75 feet (23 meters) long and 39 feet (12 meters) high. There were bigger *Brachiosaurus* skeletons there, but this was the biggest fossil skeleton to be mounted, and it held the record for decades.

| 230 | 220 | 210 | 200 | 190 | 180 | 170 | 160 | 1 |
|-----|-----|-----|-----|-----|-----|-----|-----|---|

TRIASSIC                     JURASSIC

CAMARASAU
BRACHIOSAUR

## BRACHIOSAURUS DESCRIBED

*Brachiosaurus* was a much bigger animal than either *Diplodocus* or *Apatosaurus*. Various estimates have been made of its weight, ranging between an unrealistic 180 tons and a svelte 32 tons. There are so many different ways of estimating the weight of a dinosaur and so many imponderables brought into the equation that nearly all such estimates must be regarded as somewhat spurious.

The main difference between this group of sauropods and the diplodocids is in the forequarters. The front legs are particularly long for a sauropod and the shoulders very tall. The back slopes downward from the shoulders to the hips, suggesting that the neck is held high. The vertebrae are spectacular. As in all advanced sauropods they are hollowed out to keep the weight of bone down. The neck vertebrae in particular are formed of thin lightweight struts and sheets of bone, all angled so that they would bear the weight of the neck muscles and have no surplus weight themselves. The head is not low and long, as in the diplodocids, but short and with very high nostrils and an enormous nasal cavity. This was probably a cooling mechanism, allowing cool air to pass over a large area of moist nasal membrane. The teeth were broad and chisel-shaped, and the wear on them suggests that *Brachiosaurus* went for tough, abrasive plant material as food.

## BIG BEASTS

As with Diplodocus and the other diplodocids, there is the one reliable skeleton and other tantalizing fragments of bigger relatives.

Consider the complex history of *Ultrasauros* (note the spelling), which was found in 1972, in Colorado, by dinosaur hunter Jim Jensen. The specimen consisted of a single shoulder blade that was about 15

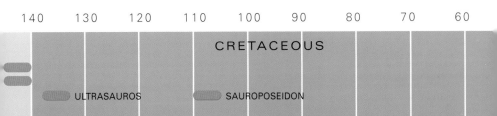

140    130    120    110    100    90    80    70    60

CRETACEOUS

ULTRASAUROS          SAUROPOSEIDON

percent bigger than the one on the Humboldt Museum's *Brachiosaurus*. He dubbed this new monster *Ultrasaurus*, but lost the right to the name before he got around to describing it scientifically. In 1983 Korean paleontologist Haang Mook Kim found a fragmentary sauropod skeleton in Korea and published its description, naming it as a new species of *Ultrasaurus*. It turned out to be a totally different kind of sauropod altogether, but the name was irrevocably attached to it. Because the rules of naming new species, Jensen had to find a new name for his specimen. He changed the spelling to *Ultrasauros*. Subsequently, it was found that this giant shoulder blade was merely a particularly large specimen of *Brachiosaurus*, so even *Ultrasauros* is not a valid dinosaur genus.

In 2000 an articulated series of four brachiosaurid neck vertebrae turned up in early Cretaceous rocks of Oklahoma. The spines on the top of the vertebrae and the pattern of the weight-saving hollows were very *Brachiosaurus*-like, but there were enough differences to show this to be a completely new animal. It was given the name *Sauroposeidon*—"lizard of the ancient Greek god of earthquakes." *Sauroposeidon* was restored as a larger version of *Brachiosaurus*—a 25 percent larger version of *Brachiosaurus*. This was the last-known of the brachiosaurid group, and probably represents the climax of the lengthening and the lightening of the neck.

**Below:** *The skeleton of* Brachiosaurus *looks a bit like that of a giraffe. Long front legs and tall shoulders form the base for a powerful neck that could reach up and browse in the high treetops.*

## THE CAMARASAURIDS

A closely related group of sauropods was the camarasaurids. Like the diplodocids and the brachiosaurids they roamed the plains of North America in late Jurassic times. They are the most abundant remains in the Morrison Formation. Specimens of *Camarasaurus* had been coming out of the bone quarries of Wyoming since 1877, but the best was found in 1925, by fossil hunter Charles Gilmore, in the quarry that eventually became the Dinosaur National Monument in Utah. It was the complete articulated skeleton of a baby. It was no bigger than a sheep, and was lying with its head thrown back and its tail curled up. It is such a beautiful specimen that it is mounted in the Carnegie Museum in Pittsburgh in exactly the position in which it was found.

For all that *Camarasaurus* is the most common sauropod in the Morrison Formation it is mostly the bones of youngsters that are found. This gave rise to the widespread misconception that *Camarasaurus* was much smaller than any of the diplodocids or the brachiosaurids. In fact, a fully-grown *Camarasaurus* was about the bulk of an *Apatosaurus*. The shape was quite different, though. The tail was much shorter and did not have the whiplash end. This itself gave *Camarasaurus* a length of 59 feet (18 meters) as opposed to the 70 feet (21 meters) of *Apatosaurus*.

The front legs were long, although not as proportionately long as those of Brachiosaurus. They were long enough to put the shoulders at the same height as the hips and so the back was more or less horizontal. The neck bones were full of holes and hollows like the other advanced sauropods, and the musculature seems to suggest that the head was held fairly high, as in a *Brachiosaurus*. The head was very large for a sauropod, and the nostril cavity enormous. This suggested to some researchers that *Camarasaurus* (and even *Brachiosaurus*) had an elephant-like trunk on the head. However, it takes more than big nostrils on a skull to prove an elephant-like trunk. There is nowhere on the skull

where trunk muscles could be attached, and anyway, with a long neck like that what need did it have for a trunk?

Elmer Riggs, who discovered *Brachiosaurus*, could see straight away that the sauropods had been land-living animals. But, such is the way of the science, the more interesting idea of sauropods being semi-aquatic animals became popular and Riggs' clearly thought through idea was ignored for more than half a century.

## FACTFILE

The *Brachiosaurus* found in East Africa at the beginning of the twentieth century was identical to that found in North America. From the same site came a whole suite of animals that were very similar to those of the Morrison—an *Allosaurus*, a diplodocid called *Dicraeosaurus*, and a stegosaur called *Kentrosaurus*. The supercontinent of Pangaea had not fully split at that time, and North America was not that far from Africa, so similar animals lived in the two places.

## Neck Vertebra of *Brachiosaurus*

**Left and below**: *The neck bones of* Brachiosaurus *were lightweight constructions of struts and flanges, keeping the weight to an absolute minimum while sacrificing none of the strength needed to support such an enormous structure.*

*The front toes had a tiptoe arrangement to add to the height of the shoulders.*

## *Brachiosaurus* hand and foot

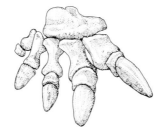

## *Brachiosaurus* skull

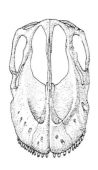
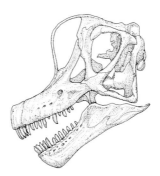

**Left**: *The significant thing about the skull of* Brachiosaurus *was the enormous area of the nostrils. The animal may have had a powerful sense of smell, or it could have been part of a cooling system for the brain.*

# Titanosaurids

We often regard the sauropods as being a peculiarly Jurassic group of beasts, with the subsequent Cretaceous scene dominated by a different group of dinosaurs altogether. We see the advanced ornithopods, such as the duckbills, as the most important Cretaceous plant-eaters. This is broadly true, but there was a group of sauropods that were present right up until the very end of the age of dinosaurs. These were the aptly named titanosaurids.

In the northern hemisphere the duckbills spread through the lowlands where newly evolved flowering plants were beginning to flourish. The surviving sauropods, on the other hand, preferred the uplands where the ancient flora of primitive conifers and cycads was still dominant.

In the southern hemisphere, however, it was a different picture. By the Cretaceous period the breakup of Pangaea was well under way. The modern continents were now distinguishable and were beginning to drift away from one another. In the southern hemisphere this breakup was continuing more slowly, with South America, Africa, India, Australia, and Antarctica forming their own group of continents a long way from those of the north. It seems that the duckbills did not really gain a foothold on these continents and there the sauropods held sway there until the end of the Mesozoic.

**Right:** *Many of the titanosaurids, like Saltasaurus (left), had backs covered in armor. Others, like Opisthoceolicaudia (right), may also have been armored, but we have no direct evidence yet.*

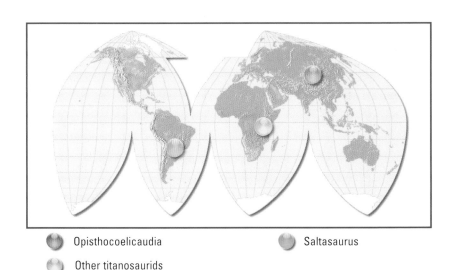

🔘 Opisthocoelicaudia          ◐ Saltasaurus

◔ Other titanosaurids

## ARMORED SAUROPODS

*Saltasaurus* from the late Cretaceous of Argentina is a typical example of a titanosaurid. A prominent feature was its back, which was covered in armor. The armor consisted of bony plates, about the size of CDs, separated by a tight groundmass of bony tubercles. The plates would have been covered in horn, possibly forming a spike. The first recorded finding of armor from the back of a sauropod dates back to 1896

| 230 | 220 | 210 | 200 | 190 | 180 | 170 | 160 | 15 |
|-----|-----|-----|-----|-----|-----|-----|-----|-----|
| TRIASSIC | | | | | JURASSIC | | | |

when Charles Depéret described *Titanosaurus* from the Upper Cretaceous of Madagascar. His account of armor on this animal was laughed at and forgotten. When *Saltasaurus* was first discovered in 1980 by Jaime Powell and José Bonaparte its armored back appeared so strange that it was regarded as a one-off aberration. Then Depéret's work was remembered. Titanosaurid armor is now turning up in places such as Malawi, and in the northern hemisphere in France and Spain.

This raises the question, why do these sauropods have armor? In the modern world tigers do not attack elephants—the elephants are too big and tigers would have little chance of killing one. It must have been the same in Mesozoic times. What meat-eating dinosaur would be able to cut through the skin of a titanosaurid, especially when that skin has been estimated as nearly 3 inches (7 centimeters) thick?

So it seems unlikely that the armor had anything to do with defense.

If we look at the skeleton of a titanosaurid, we can see a difference between it and the skeleton of an animal belonging to any of the other groups of sauropod. The backbones lack the cavernous hollows that keep the weight down. Nowhere do we see the prongs, the struts, and the bony sheets to which the back muscles are attached.

The vertebrae are quite conventional, and, to keep the weight down, they are quite small. The result of this is a backbone that is not as strong as it should be for an animal that size. Perhaps the armor was a stiffening device rather than a defensive one. Perhaps the solid covering gave strength to the back that was lacking in the backbone. After all, a crab's carapace is not just there to defend it—the muscles are attached to it as well.

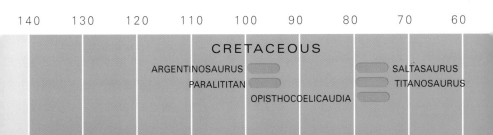

## TAIL TALE

The *Opisthocoelicaudia* is a curious titanosaurid. Its tail is quite short for a sauropod and, although there is nothing too unusual about that, it appears to have been assembled back to front. In most sauropods the vertebrae of the tail articulate with one another by means of ball-and-socket joints. Usually the ball part is in the rear of the vertebra while the socket part is at the front. This is reversed in *Opisthocoelicaudia*. The arrangement seems to have afforded this animal a particularly strong tail, probably giving it the ability to rise onto its hind legs and adopt a tripod stance, as the diplodocids could, but the heavy-fronted brachiosaurids could not.

The tails of sauropods have undergone changes during the history of paleontology. It had been assumed that the enormous tails dragged on the ground behind them as they walked. Bones on the underside of the tail of

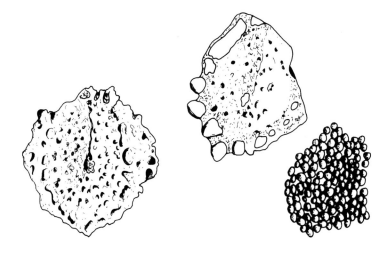

*Diplodocus* were interpreted as skids to help it to slide along. However, the drag mark of a tail was never found in the footprint track of a sauropod. All sorts of reasons were given for this, such as the idea that all footprints had been made on lakebeds and the tail was floating in the water. Now it is accepted that the tails were held clear of the ground, supported by massive tendons along the tail vertebrae.

The one skeleton that was found of *Opisthocoelicaudia*, discovered in Mongolia in 1997, led to the change in appreciation of this dinosaur. Once the tail was assembled, with its odd back-to-front articulation, the natural pose for the tail to hold was straight out behind, with no flexibility to allow it to droop to the ground.

## FACTFILE

To round off the section on sauropods on a sensational note, what was the biggest land animal that ever lived? As far as we know, it was a titanosaurid from the Upper Cretaceous of Argentina, called *Argentinosaurus*. We only know it from half a dozen back vertebrae, a rib, and a leg bone, but from these pieces we can estimate that, bearing in mind the limitations of these calculations, the living animal may have weighed something like 100 tons. Another, called *Paralititan,* from the Upper Cretaceous of Egypt, may have been about the same size. These titanosaurids saw off the age of dinosaurs with style.

**Left**: *The armor of titanosaurids consisted of CD-sized plates, that may have had a horny covering, embedded in a groundmass of densely packed bony knobbles.*

# Primitive Ornithischians

Back at the beginning of the age of dinosaurs, in the latter part of the Triassic period, a totally different group of dinosaurs evolved. The ornithischians differed from most of the saurischians that we have seen so far by the arrangement of the bones of the hip.

The saurischians had hipbones arranged like those of a lizard, with all the bones radiating away from the socket where the leg was located. The ornithischian arrangement was different in that the pubis bone, that pointed down and forward in the saurischian hip, was swept backwards and lay alongside the ischium bone. In some, an extension of the pubis bone reached forward and along the side of the body. This arrangement is similar to that found in the hipbones of a bird.

This arrangement had a significant effect it on the way the animal stood and walked. As we have seen, it takes a much bigger digestive system to support a plant-eating way of life than it does to support a meat-eating lifestyle. The sauropods were four-footed because they had to carry the heavy plant-eating innards well forward of the hipbone. In the ornithischians, which were all plant-eaters, the big plant-digesting guts could be carried well back, under the hips, between the legs. As a result, a typical ornithischian had a center of gravity that was close to the hips and, although it was a plant-eater and had a big plant-eater's body, it could still walk on its hind

**Right:** *Early in the age of dinosaurs the ornithischians evolved. These were all plant-eaters, and the early forms were quite small. They included* Lesothosaurus *(left), armoured* Scutellosaurus *(front), and fang-toothed* Heterodontosaurus *(right).*

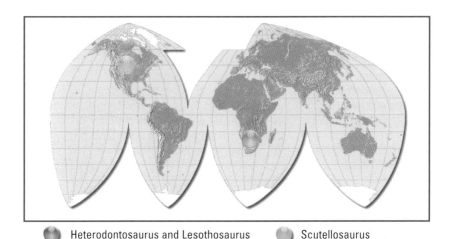

Heterodontosaurus and Lesothosaurus      Scutellosaurus

legs balanced by a heavy tail.

Some later groups of ornithischians were four-footed. These dinosaurs were covered in armor or had heavy horns—features that would preclude an active two-footed lifestyle. But the basic ornithischian was a two-footed plant-eater.

## POLITE EATERS

A less obvious difference between the saurischians and the ornithischians is the presence of an extra bone, the predentary, in the front of the lower jaw of the ornithischians.

In fact, the skull of a typical ornithischian had a number of features

230      220      210      200      190      180      170      160      15

TRIASSIC                              JURASSIC

LESOTHOSAURUS
HETERODONTOSAURUS
LYCORHINUS
SCUTELLOSAURUS

that distinguished it from that of a saurischian. As well as the extra predentary bone, there was a beak in the front of the mouth. We can tell this by the texture of the bone at the tips of the jaws—a wrinkled surface suggests that a horny structure had once grown there. The tooth row was set in from the side of the skull, leaving a gap at the side of the mouth. This suggests that the animal had cheeks, covering that gap and forming a pouch that could hold on to the food while it was being chewed. Unlike the teeth of a sauropod, the teeth of an ornithischian were well adapted for chopping, chewing, and grinding. These animals could process their food quite thoroughly before swallowing it—no need for stomach stones or a gizzard.

The most abundant group of ornithischians was the ornithopods. Not only did they have hips like the hips of a bird, but they also had bird-like feet. These were the classic two-

## FACTFILE

**Australian paleontologist Tony Thulborn suggested that heterodontosaurids slept through the hottest and most uncomfortable times of the year. The seasonal desert environment in which they lived indicated this, as did the growth pattern of the teeth. The suggestion was disputed by American palaeontologist Jim Hopson, who named one Abrictosaurus ("wide awake reptile").**

footed plant-eaters of Triassic and Jurassic times, reaching their climax at the end of the Cretaceous.

## PRIMITIVE ORNITHISCHIANS
The primitive ornithischians are a diverse bunch that cannot readily be classified. It seems as if all kinds of

| 140 | 130 | 120 | 110 | 100 | 90 | 80 | 70 | 60 |

CRETACEOUS

evolutionary lines started at that time, before the branches settled and developed into the main families. If any genus can be regarded as the typical early form, it is probably *Lesothosaurus*.

*Lesothosaurus* was about the size of a big modern lizard. It walked on its hind legs balanced by a long tail. It was a plant-eater and carried its big plant-eater's body as a potbelly between its legs. The mouth was very primitive and lacked the cheek pouches possessed by the rest of the group. The head must have been similar to the head of a modern plant-eating lizard such as an iguana.

More advanced (derived) is *Heterodontosaurus*, which is known from one of the most complete and elegant fossil skeletons ever discovered. It lay with its legs in a running posture, its arms tucked into its chest, and its tail swinging out behind—it looked like a snapshot of an agile dinosaur in action. *Heterodontosaurus* was unusual in having a number of different kinds of teeth. At the front of the mouth was a beak, as in all ornithischians. Next were some pairs of fangs, rather like the canine teeth of a dog. In fact, when the jawbone of its close relative *Lycorhinus*

was first discovered it was assumed to be the jawbone of a mammal-like reptile—the kind of thing that eventually evolved into the mammals with their wide array of different teeth. The fangs of *Heterodontosaurus* may have been possessed only by the males, and used in combat or display. Perhaps some of the fang-less relatives of *Heterodontosaurus* were actually females, rather than different genera. Behind the fangs were rows of chewing and grinding teeth, with a mouth structure that suggests cheek pouches. The jaw joint was below the line of the tooth row, an arrangement that produced good leverage for scissor-like action of the jaws.

The hands of *Heterodontosaurus* were quite big, and probably used for digging in the ground for stems and roots. There was a full compliment of five fingers on each hand, which is typical of the ornithischians. In *Heterodontosaurus* the fourth and fifth fingers were reduced, and so there were really only three fingers that were

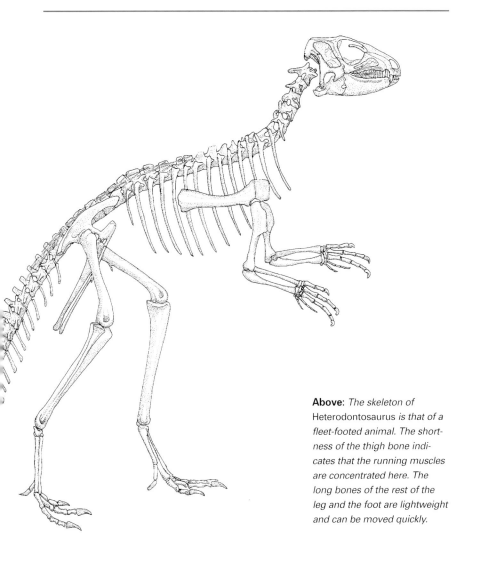

**Above:** *The skeleton of* Heterodontosaurus *is that of a fleet-footed animal. The shortness of the thigh bone indicates that the running muscles are concentrated here. The long bones of the rest of the leg and the foot are lightweight and can be moved quickly.*

functional, but this reduction was nowhere near as extreme as we see in the theropods.

## PRIMITIVE ARMOR

Another primitive ornithischian of these early times was *Scutellosaurus*. It was rather like *Lesothosaurus* in the shape of its head and the arrangement of its teeth. Its tail was particularly long—twice as long as the body and the neck together—and the hind limbs were rather short for a two-footed animal. The strange thing about this animal was the armor, over 304 pieces of plate covered its neck, back, and tail. This may account for its short hind legs. Heavy armor like this would suggest that this was not a fleet-footed animal.

Perhaps it moved about on all fours, squatting down in the dirt and presenting the armored back whenever any dangerous predator approached. Although it has many similarities to *Lesothosaurus*, the armor suggests that it is more closely related to the ancestry of the heavy armored and plated dinosaurs that were to come.

Incidentally, the bird-like hipbone arrangement was not really unique to the ornithischians. It occasionally evolved in the saurischians too. The maniraptorans had a bird-like pelvis with the pubis bone swept backward. The mysterious therizinosaurs also had this shape of hip. Of course, birds also had a bird-like hip, which evolved directly from the saurischian dinosaurs.

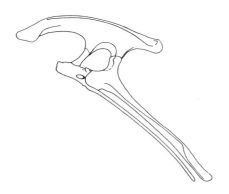

**Left:** *The hip bones are typical of ornithischians. The pubis bone does not project forward as in the lizard-like saurischians, but is swept back alongside the ischium bone. This leaves room for a bigger plant-eating gut beneath.*

**Right:** *Ornithischian hands often had the full compliment of five fingers. Their feet were very much like those of saurischians— with three functional toes.*

**Below:** *Well equiped for survival against predators, some would be swift and agile and would flee while others were moderately fleet of foot but also partly armored. Others would have used fangs and threat display*

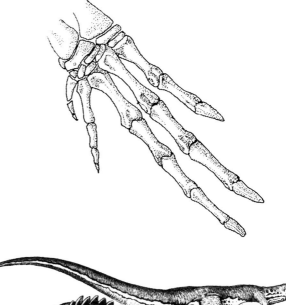

# Small Ornithopods

Soon after the ornithopods evolved, they developed into fleet footed forms. The hypsilophodontids were the gazelles of the Mesozoic. In modern zoology we find that many strategies evolved to allow plant-eating animals to escape the predators of the time and place. Some develop armor to combat the teeth and claws of the predators, some develop poison to deter them, and some develop a turn of speed to take them swiftly away from danger. The antelope and gazelles of the open plains graze peacefully, until a big cat comes on the scene, then they make off at great speed. The whole of the body shape is adapted to doing this.

## DINOSAURIAN GAZELLE

The *Hypsilophodon* is a 6½ feet (2 meters) long, peaceful browser of early Cretaceous times. It has big eyes on the side of its head, giving it a wide field of view over the surrounding landscape. Should any danger come into view it will run. Its whole leg arrangement is evolved for speed. It has a short thighbone and long shanks, and long lightweight foot bones. An arrangement like this concentrates all the running muscles at the top of the legs, around the hips. The rest of the leg is controlled by tendons, which work the feet and toes. This makes for a lightweight foot that can be moved quickly.

*Hypsilophodonts and iguanodonts had basically the same shape. The former, such as Hypsilophodon (bottom) and Dryosaurus (middle), were swift-footed sprinters, while the latter, like Tenontosaurus (top), were bigger and slower-moving.*

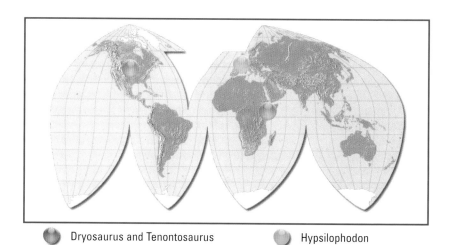

Dryosaurus and Tenontosaurus          Hypsilophodon

   Obvious though this is, it took a long time to catch on amongst paleontologists. The first *Hypsilophodon* skeleton was found in England, by Gideon Mantell (the pioneer naturalist who uncovered the mighty *Iguanodon*), in 1849. He thought that this specimen was actually a baby *Iguanodon*. Twenty years later more specimens came to light, and it was Thomas Huxley who realized that they were different from *Iguanodon* and named them *Hypsilophodon*. In 1882 James Hulke published a paper that described the skeleton of *Hypsilophodon* and came to the conclusion

230          220          210          200          190          180          170          160          15

**TRIASSIC**                                        **JURASSIC**

DRYOSAURU
DYSALOTOSAU

that it was a tree-climbing dinosaur. The reasons included the observation that the first toe of the hind foot was turned backward, as in modern perching birds, the claws were curved and looked good for grasping branches, the bones of the forearm seemed to be adapted for clutching tree trunks and the tail was stiff and straight like the stiff tails of African monkeys. Add to this the fact that the animal had the size and proportions of a modern tree kangaroo and the argument seemed above reproach. For about eighty years *Hypsilophodon* was regarded by everybody as a climbing dinosaur.

It was the work of Peter Galton in the 1960s that disproved this. He found that the first toe was not turned back after all, the toes were not particularly curved, and the forearm was no more adapted to clutching trunks than those of any other ornithopod. Galton also noted that the legs were built for fast running and the stiff tail would have

been more useful as a balance for running than for climbing.

## A WIDESPREAD GROUP

The small ornithopods, including the hypsilophodonts, were widespread animals. *Dryosaurus* of North America has a very close relative in *Dysalotosaurus* from Tanzania, one of the many fossils unearthed by a German expedition in the early years of the twentieth century. The two are so similar that many scientists regard them as the same genus. An interesting member of the group is *Leaelly-nasaura*, which comes from Victoria in Australia. Found in the 1980s, it proved that dinosaurs could have survived in contemporary arctic conditions. During the early Cretaceous perid that corner of Australia was within the Antarctic Circle. The eyes of *Leaellynasaura* were very large, leading to the suggestion that these animals were active in the long dark Antarctic night.

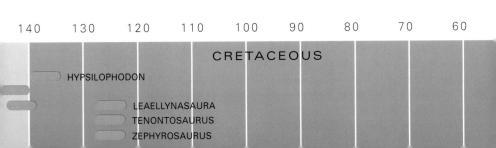

140　　130　　120　　110　　100　　90　　80　　70　　60

CRETACEOUS

HYPSILOPHODON

LEAELLYNASAURA

TENONTOSAURUS

ZEPHYROSAURUS

A dinosaur that we used to think belonged to the hypsilophodonts, but now regard as being closer to *Iguanodon*, was *Tenontosaurus*. This was very much larger than *Hypsilophodon*—about the size of a cow—and was much slower. It had a massive deep tail compared with the others and probably spent much of its time down on all fours. The tail may have been used as a solar collector rather than a balancing organ. The remains of *Tenontosaurus* outnumber those of any other dinosaur in rocks laid down on the plains of early Cretaceous Arizona, suggesting that it was one of the most abundant animals around. However they are never found fossilized in groups, which seems to indicate that they were solitary animals.

Often their remains are found with broken *Deinonychus* teeth associated with them. Evidently they represented a major part of the diet of these maniraptorans. One dismembered *Tenontosaurus* skeleton has been found with not only the scattered remains of *Deinonychus* teeth, but parts of the skeletons of four *Deinonychus* individuals. It seems that a pack of *Deinonychus* attacked a large *Tenontosaurus* that put up a much stronger fight than usual.

The result seems to have been that, although the *Tenontosaurus* was killed and eaten, it had managed to kill several of its attackers as well. The deposit seems to indicate that the dead *Deinonychus* were also eaten before the site was covered and buried by a river flood.

In the same area, and at the same time, there were more conventional hypsilophodontids. *Zephyrosaurus* was a small fleet-footed animal that looked much more like *Hypsilophodon*.

## FACTFILE

In 1993 the skeleton of a big hypsilophondont, *Thescelosaurus*, turned up in South Dakota. In 2000 it was found to contain a mineralized lump that appears to be the fossilized heart. Its structure seems to be more like that of a bird than a reptile, suggesting that these dinosaurs had a high metabolic rate and an active lifestyle.

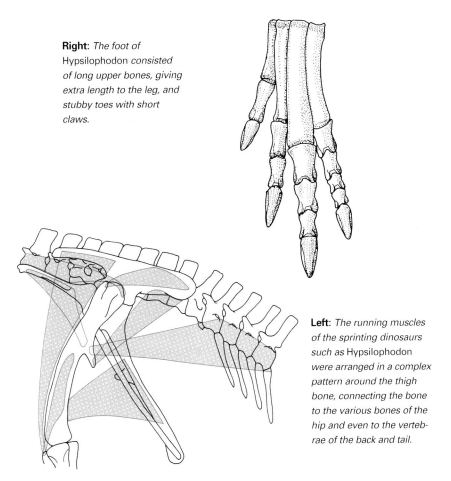

**Right:** *The foot of* Hypsilophodon *consisted of long upper bones, giving extra length to the leg, and stubby toes with short claws.*

**Left:** *The running muscles of the sprinting dinosaurs such as* Hypsilophodon *were arranged in a complex pattern around the thigh bone, connecting the bone to the various bones of the hip and even to the vertebrae of the back and tail.*

# Iguanodonts

*I*guanodon was one of the first of the dinosaurs to have been recognized and described.

The laurels for this go to the country doctor Gideon Mantell who, with his wife Mary, spent all of their spare time looking for fossils in the quarries of their native Kent in the early part of the nineteenth century. The most intriguing fossils that came to light were the bones of something that looked like an enormous reptile. William Buckland, in Oxford, was studying the theropod *Megalosaurus* at this time, so it seems that the time of dinosaur appreciation had arrived.

### A NEW KIND OF ANIMAL

The most puzzling aspect of Mantell's discovery was the teeth. They were obviously the teeth of a plant-eating animal, but, at that time, no modern plant-eating reptiles were known. The plant-eating iguana lizards from South America were not widely familiar. Mantell continued to affirm that the bones were of a big reptile and included illustrations of them and the teeth in a book entitled *The Fossils of the South Downs*, published in 1822. The teeth were dismissed by the scientific establishment of the time as the teeth of a fish. His friend and collaborator, the geologist Charles Lyell, took them to the foremost authority on comparative anatomy and fossil vertebrates, George Cuvier of Paris, who identified them as the teeth of a

*The iguanodonts, such as* Iguanodon *(bottom, left),* Camptosaurus *(bottom, right), and* Muttaburrasaurus *(top right) were an important group of plant-eaters in the early Cretaceous. They gave rise to the later duckbilled hadrosaurids, such as* Ouranosaurus *(top left)*

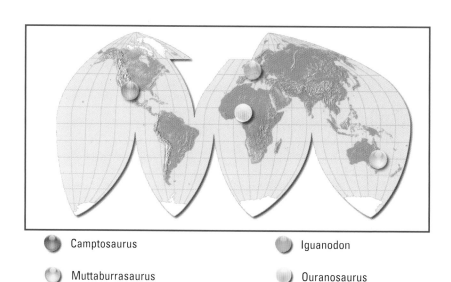

🌓 Camptosaurus

🌑 Iguanodon

🌘 Muttaburrasaurus

🌕 Ouranosaurus

rhinoceros. The appearance of an iguana on display at the Royal College of Surgeons showed that plant-eating reptiles did exist after all, and so Mantell named his big reptile *Iguanodon*, or "iguana tooth" in 1825.

*Megalosaurus* and *Iguanodon*, and parts of an armored dinosaur, *Hylaeosaurus* (also discovered by Mantell), led the most eminent British biologist of the day, Sir Richard Owen, to set up a new classification of

230    220    210    200    190    180    170    160    15

**TRIASSIC**

**JURASSIC**

animals at the meeting of the British Association for the Advancement of Science in 1841. He called this new group the "dinosauria."

## SHAPE SHIFTING

An unseemly feud developed between Owen and Mantell and it appears that the former, using the influence of his standing in the academic world, made sure that Mantell never received due credit for his discoveries. Mantell's interpretation of the fossils as having come from an animal with short front legs that habitually spent much of its time sitting upright was brushed aside. Owen saw *Iguanodon* as a big four-footed dragon-like reptile, and so it was perceived for decades. The discovery of over thirty complete Iguanodon skeletons in a coalmine in Belgium, in 1878, exonerated Mantell (long after his death).

The "kangaroo" pose of *Iguanodon*— sitting back on its hips, its knees bent, its tail along the ground, its arms in a

### FACTFILE

Athough the iguanodonts were predominantly large northern hemisphere beasts, the most primitive were small and were found in South America. *Gasparinisaura* and *Anabisetia* from Argentina were more like hypsilophodonts in size.

puppy-dog begging position, became the accepted image for about eighty years. Then, in the 1970s work by David Norman of Cambridge showed this to have been a very uncomfortable position indeed for *Iguanodon*. As a result of his work *Iguanodon* is now seen as holding its body horizontally and, as often as not, supporting its forequarters on its hands. It appears that *Iguanodon* is back on all fours, just like Owen said!

| 140 | 130 | 120 | 110 | 100 | 90 | 80 | 70 | 60 |
|---|---|---|---|---|---|---|---|---|

CRETACEOUS

IGUANODON     MUTTABURRASAURUS

CAMPTOSAURUS     OURANOSAURUS

## IGUANODON DESCRIBED

As time went on, the chewing mechanisms of the ornithopods seemed to become more and more sophisticated. The teeth of *Iguanodon* were grinding teeth, and the grinding surfaces were at an angle. As the lower jaw rose to the upper, the teeth went between the upper tooth rows. The upper jaw bones were so loosely attached to the skull that they actually moved outwards as the lower jaw came up, so giving the play for the grinding action between the sets of teeth. The cheek pouches would have held the food as it was mashed in this way.

The hand of *Iguanodon* is noteworthy. As with most ornithopods it had three fingers, but these were as versatile as a Swiss army knife. The three middle fingers were strong and had weight-bearing hooves on the ends. It was these that took the weight of the animal's forequarters as it walked. The first finger, equivalent to our thumb, had a huge horny spike. This must have been used as a defensive weapon, or as some kind of a tool to pull down branches. The fifth finger was small and prehensile. It must have been used as we use our thumbs, for manipulating plant material against the rest of the hand.

*Iguanodon* seems to have been such a good design of animal that its relatives spread all over the world. *Camptosaurus* was an earlier form that lived amongst the many types of sauropod on the plains that gave rise to the Upper Jurassic Morrison Formation in North America. *Muttaburrasaurus* was a representative from Australia.

## SAILBACK

For all that *Iguanodon* was a successful animal, its success was limited to the early part of the Cretaceous period. Toward the second half of the Cretaceous an offshoot of the *Iguanodon* line gave rise to an even more successful group. But before we deal with them, let us look at a peculiar beast that lay somewhere along this evolutionary path.

*Ouranosaurus* lived in middle Cretaceous times in northern Africa. It was very much like *Iguanodon* in build. However, along its backbone there sprouted a series of tall spines forming what looked like a bony picket fence all along the back. In life this was probably covered by skin to form a kind of a sail. The most obvious function of a sail like this would have been as a heat-exchange mechanism. The covering skin would have been filled with blood vessels. In the morning, when things were cool, *Ouranosaurus* could have stood sideways on to the rising sun, absorbing warmth and therefore becoming active early. At midday when things were hot it could have held its sail into the wind and cooled if off. This procedure would have been very effective in open semi-desert conditions—the kind of conditions we think that *Ouranosaurus* inhabited.

Another theory is that this bony fence actually supported a fatty hump, like that of a buffalo or a camel, as a food store against times of want. Again, in a semi-desert environment this would have been a good idea.

**Below**: *The* Iguanodon *skull (left) had a complex chewing mechanism. The interior of the skull (right) shows the upper jaw bone separate from the main part of the skull. The upper jaw bone was able to move independently to produce a grinding action.*

**Left**: Iguanodon's *hand had three middle fingers supporting its weight while walking on all fours, the thumb was a horny spike, possibly for defence, and the fifth finger was prehensile like a thumb. Three weight-bearing toes formed the foot of* Iguanodon. *The broad toe tips carried heavy hooves.*

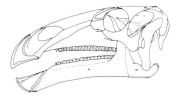

# Hadrosaurids I

The hadrosaurids were the last group of ornithopods to evolve. They developed rapidly into the most successful and diverse group of dinosaurs imaginable. They seem to have evolved in the heart of Asia and from there spread across the whole of the northern hemisphere. Their remains are found in Europe, in Asia, and most significantly, in America. There they halted, and never gained a foothold in South America, on what was then an island continent.

The first dinosaur to be discovered and described in America was *Hadrosaurus*, back in 1858. William Parker Foulke, who had heard about fossil bones being discovered earlier in a particular quarry, dug up the remains in New Jersey. These were described by the paleontologist Joseph Leidy. Leidy saw that these remains came from an animal very similar to *Iguanodon*. However, at that time the public image of *Iguanodon* was Owen's clumsy dragon-like animal, and Leidy saw that the stance of *Hadrosaurus* was nothing like that. He was of the opinion that *Hadrosaurus* spent much of its time on hind legs with its front feet clear of the ground. Although he did not know it, he was vindicating Mantell's discredited work.

*The most successful plant-eaters at the end of the age of dinosaurs were the hadrosaurids— the duckbills. Some of these (the uncrested types) had flat heads and included* Anatosaurus *(left),* Edmontosaurus *(bottom),* Bactrosaurus *(top), and* Kritosaurus *(right).*

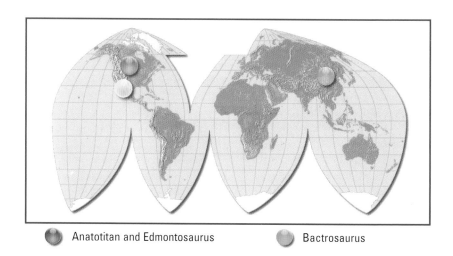

🔴 Anatotitan and Edmontosaurus   🟡 Bactrosaurus

⚪ Kritosaurus

## BONE WARS

As settlers spread west and found dinosaur skeletons in the newly claimed ground, dinosaur hunters and paleontologists also moved west, to gather the new finds. The second half of the nineteenth century was the time of the "bone wars."

The two most prominent paleontologists of the time were Othniel Charles Marsh of Yale University and Edward Drinker Cope of

| 230 | 220 | 210 | 200 | 190 | 180 | 170 | 160 | 15( |

TRIASSIC                    JURASSIC

the US Geological Survey. The two men began by working together but soon became bitter rivals. For about thirty years they exerted themselves to outdo one another in their attempts to find the biggest and best discoveries. They poached one another's staff and their excavation teams engaged in open warfare. They sabotaged sites so that their rivals could not get at them. It was a disgraceful way for scientists to behave, but it was the spur that pushed the science onward. After thirty years of this the result was the naming of about 150 new dinosaurs. Among these were many of the hadrosaurids.

## EDMONTOSAURUS—
## THE TYPICAL ONE

*Edmontosaurus* is probably the best known of the hadrosaurids. The remains of hundreds of individuals have been found. The skeleton was very much like that of *Iguanodon*, with the heavy hind legs and the more lightweight front legs.

### FACTFILE

The discovery of a whole nesting site of hadrosaurids in Montana in the 1970s proved that these dinosaurs had a complex herd structure and looked after their young as they grew. The hadrosaurid in question was *Maiasaura*, the "good mother lizard." It seems that they returned to the same site year after year.

The hand, however, was only four-fingered. The first finger, with the spectacular thumb spike, was entirely atrophied away. The tail was deep and stiff, the vertebrae were cemented together by tendons that had turned to bone. The biggest difference between it and *Iguanodon* was the shape of the head. The beak at the front was broad and flat like the beak of a duck, and gave rise to the popular term for the group—the duckbills.

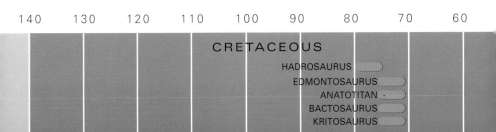

| 140 | 130 | 120 | 110 | 100 | 90 | 80 | 70 | 60 |
|---|---|---|---|---|---|---|---|---|

CRETACEOUS

HADROSAURUS
EDMONTOSAURUS
ANATOTITAN ·
BACTOSAURUS
KRITOSAURUS

Some of the remains are very well preserved and include specimens that have skin. These show that the hide was quite thin and leathery, and studded with tubercles. However, the presence of the skin led to misunderstandings. Around the hand the skin looked as though it formed a mitten around the finger bones. This was interpreted as a web to help in swimming. This, together with the duck-like beak and the deep tail like the swimming tail of a crocodile, gave rise to the idea that the hadrosaurids were aquatic animals.

## A NEW VIEW

The work of many paleontologists, including Robert Bakker, in the 1970s proved otherwise. The tail was not flexible like a crocodile's, and did not have attachments for muscles that would be needed in a swimming organ. The beak was not adapted for soft water weed like the beak of a duck, but more for scraping needles from conifer trees. The web on the hand was not a web at all, but a sort of a weight-bearing pad to help it to walk. The hadrosaurids are now accepted as entirely land-living animals.

The jaws showed the same chewing action as *Iguanodon*, with the upper jawbones that moved outwards to help in the chewing action. However, the mouth of a hadrosaurid had many more teeth. They grew constantly and formed a continuous abrasive surface. A complex structure of enamel ensured that

**Above**: *The hadrosaurid skeleton was very similar to that of the iguanodonts, with a heavy tail balancing the forequarters. The arms were strong, allowing the animal to walk on all fours when it wished, but it could also rear up to grasp food from trees.*

they wore irregularly and constantly presented a rough surface for grinding. As they dropped out new ones were added to the underside of the grinding surface. At any one time a hadrosaurid would have had hundreds of teeth in its mouth. This was an adaptation for eating very tough food.

## A NOISY LOT

Another interpretation of the broad duck-like skull is the possibility of there being some kind of a noise-producing organ on it. The flat surface may have supported a flap of skin over the nostrils. Such a flap could have been inflated and used to make deep booming sounds, like the inflatable throat of a frog. Some of these hadrosaurids had small crests of solid bone on the head as well. Such a crest could have supported an even larger flap of skin. In this way the herds of hadrosaurids could communicate with one another through the deep deciduous forest that covered much of North America at the end of the Cretaceous period.

# Hadrosaurids II

As the hadrosaurids developed, diversified, and spread all over the northern hemisphere, they split into two major groups. One was the flat-headed group that we have just covered. The other group, covered here, specialized in the most fantastic head ornaments.

Let us look at the most extreme form first. *Parasaurolophus* had a crest that swept upward and backward from the back of the skull. The crest more than doubled the length of the skull. It was developed from the nasal bones and was constructed as a series of hollow tubes, all folded back on one another. It was a most spectacular structure, but there have been a few interpretations of what it was used for.

## WHY THE CREST?

One interpretation is that the crest is a display structure. Now, when you hear paleontologists talk about "display structures" it is like listening to archaeologists saying that a particular artifact performed a "ritual function"—in other words they just do not know. Yes, it is very likely that dinosaurs used display structures for signaling to

The crested hadrosaurids,
such as Tsintaosaurus
(back left), Saurolophus
(front left), Corythosaurus
(back right), and
Parasaurolophus (front
right), were distinguished
from one another by their
head ornament.

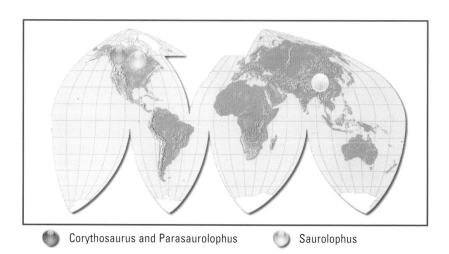

🔵 Corythosaurus and Parasaurolophus    ⚪ Saurolophus

⚪ Tsintaosaurus

other members of their species, or to strangers, but it cannot be proved. As a result, whenever a structure crops up on a dinosaur, and there is no obvious reason for its presence, it is usually explained as a display structure.

Something big on the head like this would make an ideal display structure since it could have been seen from a long way away. It is possible that the long crest of *Parasaurolophus* supported a web of skin between it and

230    220    210    200    190    180    170    160    15

**TRIASSIC**                            **JURASSIC**

the back of the neck, so increasing the area that could be seen from afar. All of this makes good sense.

Another interpretation goes back to the time when it was thought that the hadrosasurids were aquatic animals. If they lived in the water and foraged under the surface for waterweeds, then the crest of *Parasaurolophus* might be a kind of a snorkel, bringing air from the surface down to the nostrils. This does not work, since there is no hole in the end of the crest, as a snorkel would have. Then perhaps it was a kind of an aqualung, holding a reserve of air that could be called upon while submerged. This won't do as a theory either. The miniscule volume of air trapped in the crest would not have made it worthwhile. Perhaps it was a kind air lock, to prevent water from flooding into the nasal cavities? We now know that these animals were not aquatic and so these are all dead-end theories.

On the other hand, the crest may have had something to do with the sense of smell, carrying large areas of scent detectors. Or perhaps they carried salt glands to help to regulate the body chemistry of these dinosaurs.

A more likely idea is that it was like the big nostril areas on some of the sauropods, as a means of cooling the brain. Air circulating through moist membranes in these tubes could carry away excess heat and prevent brain damage in hot weather.

## FACTFILE

The curve of a hadrosaurid's neck is reminiscent of that of the neck of a horse. This has led some palaeontologists, notably Stephen Czerkas, to suggest that a hadrosaur's neck would have been backed up by strong muscles connecting it to its back, producing a deep neck like that of a horse.

| 140 | 130 | 120 | 110 | 100 | 90 | 80 | 70 | 60 |

CRETACEOUS

PARASAUROLOPHUS

CORYTHOSAURUS

LAMBEOSAURUS

TSINTAOSAURUS

The currently held view is that this remarkable crest was used for making a noise. Grunts sent up from the nostrils reverberating through the convoluted hollow tubes would have made a very distinctive sound. The actual sound has been generated by means of computer and sounds like a bass trombone—an ideal sound for penetrating thick forests and used for communicating with others of their species. It could have served the same function as the postulated flaps of skin on the snouts of the flat-headed hadrosaurids.

## A VARIETY OF HEAD SHAPES

The other crested hadrosaurids had different crests, but the rest of the animal was completely interchangeable. Another known *Parasaurolophus* had a smaller crest,

which was shorter and more tightly curved. Paleontologists are undecided as to whether this actually represented a different species of *Parasaurolophus*, or a female of the established species, or even a different genus altogether.

An intriguing suggestion is that the curved crest of *Parasaurolophus* worked as a kind of a plow, for deflecting thick vegetation as the animal crashed through thick undergrowth. It does seem that the tip of the crest could fit into a notch that was present in the backbone in the region of the shoulders, giving the whole animal a streamlined appearance. However, this would not work for any of the other crested hadrosaurids, as the shapes of the crests were extremely varied.

*Corythosaurus* is a well-known crested hadrosaurid. Its crest was semicircular and orientated fore-and-

 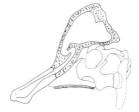 

aft, giving the impression of the plumed crest on an ancient helmet. The inside of this crest had a complex series of breathing tubes and hollow spaces. Again there are different sizes of crest amongst *Corythosaurus* individuals, giving rise to similar uncertainties about classification.

*Lambeosaurus* has a crest that seemed to have been formed of two parts—a squarish part that occupied the same space as *Corythosaurus's* semicircular one, and a solid prong that stuck out backwards.

*Tsintaosasurus* had a tall crest that pointed upward and forward. There was a body of scientific opinion that suggested that this was actually a mistake in the reconstruction of the skeleton in Institute of Vertebrate Paleontology and Paleoanthropology in Beijing, and that the crest should have been directed backward. Subsequent research has shown however, that this is the correct orientation.

The hadrosasurids were amongst the last dinosaurs to evolve and to flourish before the extinction of the whole dinosaur group at the end of the Cretaceous period.

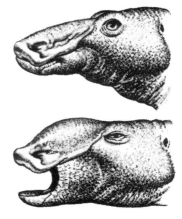

**Right:** *In the crested hadrosaurs the noise-producing mechanism was in the hollow tubes of the nasal passages. In the crest-less types sound was probably produced from an inflatable pouch over the nostrils.*

**Left to right:** Lambo-saurus, Corythosaurus, *and* Parasaurolophus *skulls., showing the internal annatomy of the crest.*

# Primitive Horned Dinosaurus

The ornithopods represented a quite conservative group of the ornithischians. Throughout their history they looked very much like their ancestors. In contrast, the rest of the ornithischians were quite diverse.

The ceratopsians were the horned dinosaurs— the rhinoceros-shaped ones with the flamboyant neck frills and the serious-looking head horns. In a simplified way we can see how they evolved from their two-footed plant-eating ancestors. Imagine a two-footed plant-eater like a primitive ornithopod. Now let it specialize in browsing tough plants like cycads. It needs particularly strong jaws and a big beak. The muscles needed to work these strong jaws need to be anchored somewhere, and so a bony shelf develops around the back of the skull. As  time passes the jaws become heavier and heavier and the bony shelf becomes bigger and bigger, and eventually evolves into a bony shield that covers the neck.

A heavy head like this makes the originally two-

The line that was to produce the spectacular horned dinosaurs of the end of the age of dinosaurs started with animals that were like ornithopods, but with heavier heads. Psittacosaurus *(right) is* typical of these. Eventually the heads became bigger and developed the typical armored shield, as in Protoceratops *(left).*

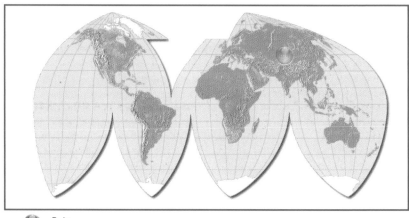

Psittacosaurus

footed animal unbalanced and so down it goes on to all fours. Now we have the basic shape of a ceratopsian.

## PARROT LIZARD
Looking at the fossil record we can almost see the stages of this evolution. *Psittacosaurus* was, to all intents and

purposes, a two-footed plant-eating ornithischian dinosaur. It used to be classed as an ornithopod, closely related to *Hypsilophodon*. The two-legged stance, the big body balanced by the heavy tail—the characteristics were all there. However, the head was different. There was a big beak and a

| 230 | 220 | 210 | 200 | 190 | 180 | 170 | 160 | 15 |
|---|---|---|---|---|---|---|---|---|
| | TRIASSIC | | | | | JURASSIC | | |

ridge around the back of the skull, giving it a peculiar parrot-like appearance. Indeed, its name means "parrot lizard." Inside the upper beak was an extra bone—the rostral bone. All the ceratopsians had this. There have been many specimens of *Psittacosaurus* found, perhaps representing many different species, all in Asia. Evidently the ceratopsians evolved in Asia before migrating to North America where they came to their climax at the end of the Cretaceous period.

An interesting modern discovery shows that at least one species of *Psittacosaurus* had porcupine-like spines on the tail. Whether or not these extended over the whole body is unknown, and their purpose can only be guessed at.

Other primitive ceratopsians have been found in Asia, and they all seem to be little rabbit-sized animals that, despite their heavy heads, scampered about on their hind legs. These bear such names as *Archaeoceratops* and *Gracilliceratops*, indicating their ancestral positions and their lightweight build.

## THE SHEEP OF THE CRETACEOUS

Also from Asia comes *Protoceratops*. In view of the number that have been found in the Gobi desert, it has been called the sheep of the Cretaceous. Even in late Cretaceous times the Gobi region was arid, with dust storms frequent. The many remains of *Protoceratops* are the result of their having been buried in collapsing sand dunes or swirling dust clouds.

The *Protoceratops* skull is quite distinctive. The beak is huge and narrow, and the cheekbones flare out, before the neck shield rises from the rear. There is a theory that the abundance of the big-beaked skulls in Central Asia actually gave rise to the myth of the gryphon—the fabulous

| 140 | 130 | 120 | 110 | 100 | 90 | 80 | 70 | 60 |
|-----|-----|-----|-----|-----|-----|-----|-----|-----|

CRETACEOUS

LEPTOCERATOPS

ARCHAEOCERATOPS        GRACILLICERATOPS

PSITTACOSAURUS                              PROTOCERATOPS

MONTANACERATOPS

beast with the body of a lion and the forequarters of an eagle. Certainly the fossils stand out spectacularly along the ancient trade routes known from ancient times.

It was this abundance that took Roy Chapman Andrews and a team from the American Museum of Natural History in New York into the area in the early 1920s. There he uncovered a vast array of new dinosaurs, including the ubiquitous *Protoceratops*. He also discovered the first dinosaur eggs, and misinterpreted those as belonging to the horned dinosaur. Nevertheless, there is plenty of evidence from that region of *Protoceratops* family life. Skeletons have been found for all stages of growth, allowing us to see how this animal developed throughout life. The youngest have very large eye-sockets, which is common to all baby animals, and the neck shield is a mere bracket at the back of the skull. The skull is very narrow at this stage. As the skull grows it begins to fill out, with the cheekbones beginning to enlarge. At about half grown we begin to see the development of two distinct groups, probably different sexes, which are distinguished by the shape of the skull. Very rarely is the skull of any dinosaur so abundant that we can follow the ontogeny (development of the individual) of the species.

## A DEVELOPING GROUP

The teeth of the ceratopsians were different from the teeth of the ornithopods. They were not designed for grinding but for chopping. The blades of the teeth scissored past one another, powered by the immense jaw muscles, and the food held in the cheek pouches would have been cut to tiny fragments. However, this was not as efficient as the grinding action of the ornithopods and so there must have

---

## FACTFILE

*Psittacosaurus* could not have been the direct ancestor of the rest of the ceratopsians. In the several species of *Psittacosaurus* the outer fingers of the hand have been lost, so that they are effectively three-fingered. The forefeet of the later ceratopsians have the full complement of five fingers.

been some other mechanism for breaking it down. Perhaps they had complex stomachs like cows and chewed the cud, or perhaps they resorted to the stomach stones of the sauropods.

Once they had evolved on the Asian landmass, the ceratopsians migrated to North America. The history of the ceratopsians in Asia seems to end at that point and the story taken up in North America. Primitive ceratopsians, very similar to *Protoceratops* and including *Leptoceratops* and *Montanaceratops* then flourished there. But these were quite minor compared with the spectacular beasts that were to follow.

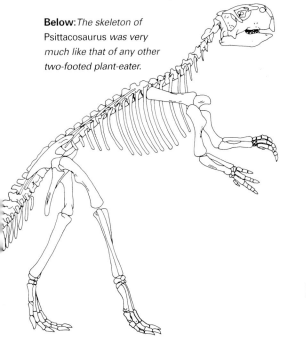

**Below:** *The skeleton of* Psittacosaurus *was very much like that of any other two-footed plant-eater.*

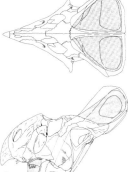

**Below:** *The neck shield of* Protoceratops *evolved to hold the massive jaw muscles that it needed to eat the tough cycad leaves that were its main foodstuff.*

# Advanced Horn Heads

In late Cretaceous North America, on fern-covered plains, with mountains in the distance, deciduous trees here and there, coniferous forests on uplands, there would be herds of big four-footed animals with huge shields around their necks and wicked horns sprouting from their heads

Big rhinoceros-like animals migrated in herds, with the seasons, between the area of Alaska and that of the Mid-West. Different herds of different horned dinosaurs kept themselves to themselves, challenging one another as they passed, and recognizing each other by the different arrangement of shields and horns. Resembling the herds of antelope and gazelle on the savannahs of today, each animal looked roughly the same but the species differentiated by their head ornamentation.

Two main branches of the advanced ceratopsians are recognized, distinguished by the head arrangement. They all had the shield and they had up to three horns on the face. For the purposes of this description we can regard them as the short-shielded and the long-shielded ceratopsians.

## SHORT SHIELDS

The short-shielded ceratopsians tended to have a single horn on the nose. Any horns above the eyes were quite small. *Styracosaurus*, an example of the short-shielded type, had a monumental horn on the

The horned dinosaurs, such as Styracosaurus *(bottom right)*, Chasmosaurus *(far left)*, Torosaurus *(front)*, Anchiceratops *(middle)*, and Pentaceratops *(back)*, all had similar body plans, but they differed from one another by the arrangement of horns on the face.

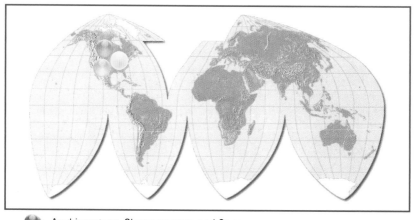

 Anchiceratops, Chasmosaurus, and Styracosaurus

 Torosaurus

 Pentacerotops

nose that thrust up and forward. The shield was quite small, but this was compensated by a whole array of horns that protruded from its rim. The nose horn would have been used as a weapon, but the shield horns were probably there for display and intimidation.

The advanced ceratopsians had an enormous beak and unique double-rooted teeth. The teeth worked with a powerful chopping action and,

| 230 | 220 | 210 | 200 | 190 | 180 | 170 | 160 | 15◖ |

TRIASSIC

JURASSIC

as usual, the food was held in cheek pouches while it was being processed. The jaw muscles were attached to the underside of the neck shield.

The body was heavy and rhinoceros-like, the pillar-like legs held beneath the body. The hind feet were broad and had four toes, only three of which were functional and reached the ground. The front feet had five toes, but again only three of them were of any use. The walking toes were furnished with heavy hooves. The tail was thick and held clear of the ground. All the advanced ceratopsians were built like this. As with the duckbills, the bodies were almost interchangeable, but the horns and shields differed.

*Styracosaurus* was not alone in having horns on the shield, but in none of the others were the horns quite so spectacular. *Centrosaurus* had little hook-like horns high up on the shield. *Einiosaurus* had a pair of horns that swept right back. *Achelousaurus* had a

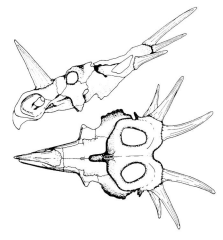

**Above:** Styracosaurus *had a single nose horn and an array of horns around the shield.*

pair of horns that curved outward. They nearly all had the single horn on the nose, but *Pachyrhinosaurus* had only a bony lump on the face. Perhaps this was used as a battering ram, or perhaps it formed the base of a structure that was made of horn but

| 140 | 130 | 120 | 110 | 100 | 90 | 80 | 70 | 60 |

CRETACEOUS

STYRACOSAURUS

ANCHICERATOPS

TOROSAURUS

CHASMOSAURUS

PENTACEROTOPS

# FACTFILE

**Some paleontologists believe that the bony lump on the head of *Pachyrhinosaurus* was actually the base for a huge horn made of keratin, like the horn of a modern rhinoceros. Rhinoceros horn does not fossilize, and the remains of fossil rhinoceroses show only a pad of bone where the horn was attached.**

had no bony core—like the horn of a rhinoceros. Until the 1980s there were only two known skulls of *Pachyrhinosaurus*. Paleontologists were coming to believe that they represented the diseased skulls of some other ceratopsian, in which the nose horn had been broken off and replaced by a mass of scar tissue. Then a bone bed with the skeletons of over two thousand *Pachyrhinosaurus* individuals, of all ages and stages of growth was found. Evidently a vast herd of these was migrating when it was caught in a flash flood as it crossed a shallow river and many of them perished. Similar tragedies strike wildebeest today as they cross the African plains in their annual migration.

Other bone beds have since been found, and by looking at all stages of the growth of individuals in the herd it was quite apparent that all short-shielded ceratopsians, whether *Pachyrhinosaurus*, *Styracosaurus*, or whatever, all looked identical until they were adults. Only then, when they were sexually mature, did they develop the distinctive horns and shield ornaments. A few genera of ceratopsians have been based on the finds of individual juvenile animals. As they all looked identical until they were mature, this could be a rather spurious exercise.

## LONG SHIELDS

The long-shielded ceratopsians had the same body plan, but the heads were different. The shields were much bigger, covering the neck and lying over the shoulders. They tended to emphasize the horns above the eyes rather than the single horn on the nose. They had an enormous nostril behind the powerful beak. This was probably mostly covered with skin and flesh in life. Unfortunately there have been no bone beds discovered that contained long-shielded ceratopsians, so we cannot tell if they showed the same pattern of growth as the short-shielded types—with the youngsters being identical until they became mature.

There are very large hollows, or sinuses, inside the skull just over the brain. Paleontologists have interpreted

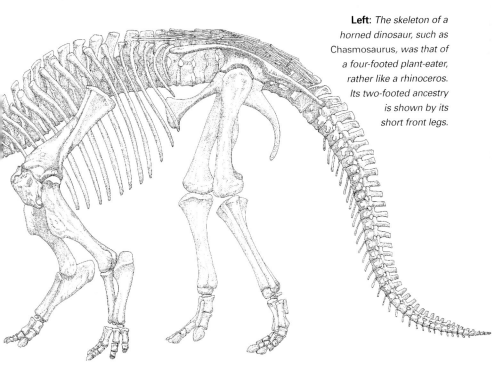

**Left:** *The skeleton of a horned dinosaur, such as* Chasmosaurus, *was that of a four-footed plant-eater, rather like a rhinoceros. Its two-footed ancestry is shown by its short front legs.*

these as a kind of a shock absorber. During battle, when these horned beasts were charging each other, the impact of two shields must have been terrific. Anything that would cushion the little brain would be an advantage. Modern goats and bison have similar sinuses below their horns, for exactly the same reason.

*Chasmosaurus* was typical. The shield was so big that, when viewed from the front it almost looked like a sail, especially when compared with the narrowness of the face. It was quite a lightweight structure too—a pair of huge holes took up most of this area of the skull. In life these holes would have been covered in skin. Most likely the skin here was brightly colored. What is the use of having a big area of body like that if you cannot use it for showing off? There has always been the assumption that the shield of a ceratopsian was used for protection, but the lightweight nature of the *Chasmosaurus* shield suggests that it had a different function entirely. Perhaps it was a signaling device. There were three horns, but none of them was particularly big. It must have used its shield for intimidation or defense. *Chasmosaurus* was found in

1914 by Lawrence Lambe of the Geological Survey of Canada. He named it *Protorosaurus*, meaning "ancestor of Torosaurus" (see below) but that name was already in use, for a little lizard-like thing from Europe, so he had to find another. He settled on *Chasmosaurus* referring to the chasms in the neck shield.

## OTHER LONG-SHIELDS

*Anchiceratops* had a tall shield, like *Chasmosaurus*, but the openings were smaller. It had little horn-like spikes on the rear margin of the shield, but none along the sides. *Chasmosaurus* had them all the way around.

*Pentaceratops* had a name that meant "five-horned face." This is something of a misnomer. It only had three horns. However, the edges of the shield in the cheek area were drawn out into a pair of points that looked like horns. In life they may have been covered in horn as well.

The longest shield belongs to *Torosaurus*. Its shield was so long that it gave the animal the biggest skull known of any land animal—a length of 8$\frac{1}{2}$ feet (2.6 meters). One of the first of the ceratopsians to be found, it was one of the last of the dinosaurs.

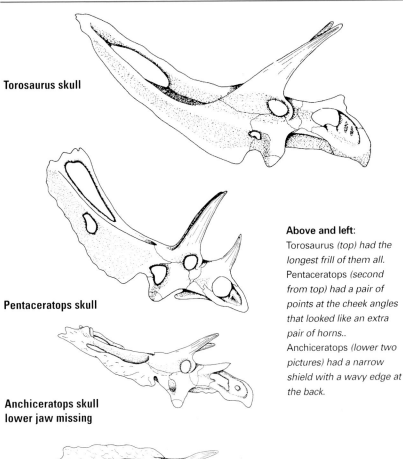

**Torosaurus skull**

**Pentaceratops skull**

**Anchiceratops skull lower jaw missing**

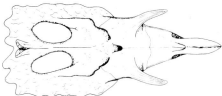

**Above and left**:
Torosaurus *(top) had the longest frill of them all.* Pentaceratops *(second from top) had a pair of points at the cheek angles that looked like an extra pair of horns..* Anchiceratops *(lower two pictures) had a narrow shield with a wavy edge at the back.*

# The Biggest Horned Dinosaur

The animal that defines the ceratopsians is without doubt *Triceratops*. It was the first to have been discovered and, because of its rather specialized build, led to a century of confusion about the classification of the horned dinosaurs.

The history starts badly. The first remains to come to scientific attention consisted of a pair of horn cores, uncovered in Colorado in 1887. When shown to Othniel Charles Marsh he pronounced them to be from an extinct giant bison, which he named *Bison alticornis*. Complete skulls came to light soon afterward and Marsh revised his identification,

**Right:** *The biggest of the horned dinosaurs was the majestic* Triceratops—*30 feet (nine meters) long and equipped with three massive horns on the face.*

changing the name to *Triceratops alticornis*.

The sheer size of *Triceratops* sets it apart from the rest of the horned dinosaur clan. It reached a length of 30 feet (9 meters) and probably weighed something like 5.5 tons. A third of its length consisted of the huge head with its solid shield and brow horns that projected forward beyond the beak. Usually dinosaur skulls are rare, falling apart and scattering soon after death,

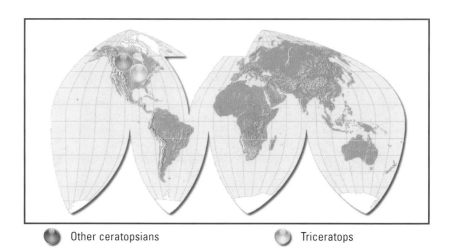

<table>
<tr><td>Other ceratopsians</td><td>Triceratops</td></tr>
</table>

but in the case of *Triceratops* the skull is so thick and heavy and sturdy that its fossils are reasonably common.

## A DIFFERENT BEAST

The other main difference between *Triceratops* and the other horned dinosaurs is the fact that the shield has no holes—it is just a solid mass. When the other ceratopsians, such as *Torosaurus*, were discovered shortly afterwards paleontologists regarded the holes in their shields as something aberrant—something that made these animals different from the rest of the group. However, not long after, it

| 230 | 220 | 210 | 200 | 190 | 180 | 170 | 160 | 15 |
|-----|-----|-----|-----|-----|-----|-----|-----|-----|

TRIASSIC · · · · · · · · · · · · · · · · · · JURASSIC

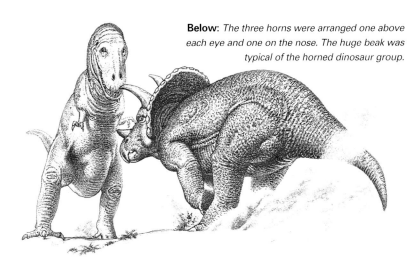

**Below:** *The three horns were arranged one above each eye and one on the nose. The huge beak was typical of the horned dinosaur group.*

appeared that *Triceratops* was the only member of the group that did not have the holes, and that this was the aberrant one. Many of the skulls of *Triceratops* had significant differences between them. Some had a big horn on the nose, while some had a little horn. Some had brow horns that stuck upward while others had brow horns that extended forward. Some had long snouts; some had short snouts. Some had deep faces; some had low faces. As a result these different shapes were assigned to different species of *Triceratops*, and at one time about fifteen species were acknowledged.

This illustrates a divergence of philosophy among paleontologists

| 140 | 130 | 120 | 110 | 100 | 90 | 80 | 70 | 60 |

CRETACEOUS

TRICERATOPS

when it comes to the classification of extinct animals. In the modern world we can define a species by practical criteria. If one animal can breed with another they are of the same species—as easy as that. This is something that cannot be ascertained from fossils. Fossil taxonomists can be regarded either as "splitters" or as "lumpers." Those of the former camp see just about every new discovery as belonging to a different species. Those of the latter like to combine groups into as few species as possible, regarding their differences as transient and unimportant. So it was with *Triceratops*. It the early part of the twentieth century there were a large number of *Triceratops* species—*Triceratops horridus, T. flabellatus, T. galeus. T. serratus, T. hatcheri* and so on, all defined by differences in the skull shape. Nowadays the lumpers hold sway. There are currently only two species of *Triceratops* that are generally regarded as valid. *T. horridus* was the more abundant and the largest, while *T. prorsus* was somewhat smaller. Some lumpers go further, regarding the two species as merely the male and female of *T. horridus*. All the other species that were described in the past now belong to one or other of these. The exception,

> # FACTFILE
>
> **The horns of *Triceratops*, and indeed the rest of the ceratopsians, would have been much longer in life than they appear on the fossils. The preserved horns are merely the bony cores—they would have been covered by keratin sheaths that must have projected far beyond the tips of the cores.**

however, is *T. hatcheri*. This has been shown to be so different (it has only the two brow horns) that it is now given its own genus. It is now known as *Diceratops hatcheri*.

There is the issue of where *Triceratops*, the biggest and the best known of the ceratopsians, actually fit into the classification and evolution of horned dinosaurs. Was it a short-shielded type, but with an unusually long shield? Or was it a long-shielded type with a bigger nose horn than usual? Current thinking leans to the latter idea.

## ONE FROM MANY
For all that dozens of skulls of *Triceratops* have been found, we have never come across a complete

skeleton. The skeletons we see mounted in museums throughout the world are actually composites, consisting of bones from several specimens—or at least the casts of these bones. The one in the American Museum of Natural History in New York is a mount consisting of four specimens from two states—Wyoming and Montana. Perhaps the most famous mounted *Triceratops* is the one in the Smithsonian Institute in Washington DC. It was the first mounted skeleton of the beast and was unveiled in 1904.

By the 1990s, however, it was looking rather the worse for wear. The steel framework was reacting with the mineral in the fossil bones and the specimen was deteriorating badly. A project was started to replace it with a virtual skeleton. Each bone was measured, scanned and fed into a computer. The sizes of the contributing skeletons did not quite match in the original, and so these were adjusted in the virtual version. The result, shown in 2002, was the most accurate reconstruction yet, albeit only in the computer. It has proved to be a valuable tool in studying the anatomy and physiology of the horned dinosaurs. A program has been run that shows how the skeleton, and by extension the original animal, could walk in its migrations across the North American plains.

**Left**: *The horned dinosaurs were gregarious, they traveled about in herds. It may well be that they defended their young in a protective circle, horns pointing outwards.*

# Pachycephalosaurids

Closely related to the ceratopsians were the pachycephalosaurids—the boneheads.

They used to be regarded as a division of the ornithopod group. Indeed, they must have looked very much like ornithopods, with their big plant-eaters' bodies supported on two legs balanced by the heavy tail. It was in the head that they differed. Each one had a bony lump on the top of the skull, which ranged from a slight thickening in the primitive forms, to a massive bony dome in the more advanced types. Around the back of the skull were bony knobs and spikes that probably supported horny ornaments. More recent studies have thrown up more differences. The tail was stiffened by a series of interlocking bony tendons, making it as stiff and straight as a plank. The base of the tail was broad and expanded by a series of ribs that extended well to the rear of the hips. This all suggests that the tails were used as props as the animals sat down—rather like a kangaroo. Admittedly there are few skeletal remains of pachycephalosaurids found, and these general observations may only apply to a few. The skulls, on the other hand, were made of quite solid chunks of bone, and so, like those of ceratopsians, they are more common than those of other dinosaurs. Many skulls have been found, badly worn and eroded, in sea sediments. The implication is that they lived well inland, possibly in mountainous areas, and the heavy skulls had undergone a long

The boneheads were close relatives of the horned dinosaurs. They ranged in size from goat-sized animals like Stegoceras (right) and Homalocephale (left), to giants like Pachycephalosaurus (middle).

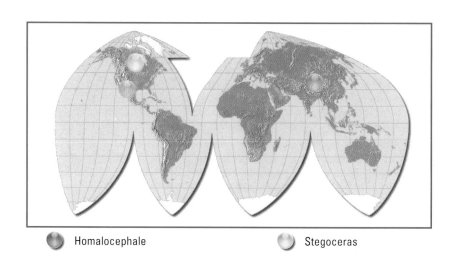

● Homalocephale ● Stegoceras

● Pachycephalosaurus

journey down mountain streams and rivers to reach their final resting places.

**A RANGE OF TYPES**

The earliest known is *Yaverlandia* from the Lower Cretaceous of the Isle of Wight. It was about the size of a rabbit and had a slight thickening of the top of the head. *Yaverlandia*, and some other primitive forms, had prominent canine teeth in the front of the lower jaw that fitted into a notch in the

230   220   210   200   190   180   170   160   15

TRIASSIC                          JURASSIC

upper—not unlike the earlier heterodontosaurids.

*Homalocephale* from the Upper Cretaceous of central Asia was a little larger and also showed a thickening of the skull, though it did not have the rounded dome of the later types. It also had a series of bony tubercles that ran along the side and across the back of the skull.

The first discovery of a pachycephalosaurid was by Lawrence Lambe in the Upper Cretaceous rocks of Alberta. He described two skulls to which he gave the name *Stegoceras*—"roof horn." At first he regarded them as belonging to a kind of ceratopsian, so anticipating their current classification. The first partial skeleton came to light in 1924 when paleontologist Charles Gilmore described remains found a few years earlier by George Sternberg at the Red Deer River. So fragmentary were the original remains that they were identified for a long time as *Troodon*.

## FACTFILE

There is a possibility that the pachycephalosaurids may not have been egg-layers, but may have borne their young alive. The hip bones of the group are particularly wide, and this has been interpreted by some paleontologists as an adaptation to allow for the passage of a baby animal.

Now, as we know, *Troodon* was actually a fleet-footed hunting theropod, very different from any boneheaded dinosaurs. To date, *Stegoceras* is the most complete bonehead known.

An oddity was *Stygimoloch* from the topmost Cretaceous of Montana. The name, meaning "horned devil from the river of death in the underworld" is not an allusion to its lifestyle but to the fact that it was found in the Hell Creek

| 140 | 130 | 120 | 110 | 100 | 90 | 80 | 70 | 60 |
|-----|-----|-----|-----|-----|----|----|----|----|

CRETACEOUS

YAVERLANDIA

HOMALOCEPHALE

STEGOCERAS

STYGIMOLOCH

PACHYCEPHALOSAURUS

Formation—a sequence of river sandstones that contains the last of the dinosaurs that ever existed. *Stygimoloch* had a series of spectacular horns that sprouted sideways and backward from the back of the skull.

Most of these animals ranged from rabbit-size to goat-size. Only in one known form did the group aspire to the sizes of some of the other dinosaurs. *Pachycephalosaurus* gave its name to the whole group, and is known from a few skulls from Montana, Wyoming, and South Dakota. These skulls were up over 2 feet (62 centimeters) long and had an extremely high dome above the eyes. They also had small horns over the snout, adding to their bizarre appearance.

## BONEHEADED LIFESTYLES

How did these animals live? What was their lifestyle? These are questions that have exercised Paleontological minds for decades. The most popular opinion is that they lived like mountain goats. The suggestion that they lived far from the sea encourages this. If they roamed the mountain flanks in herds there would have been frequent bouts of sparring amongst the males, to see which one would lead the herd. Modern mountain goats do this by means of ritual fights, in which the males crash heads to see which is the stronger. A Mountain goat's horn structure is adapted for this sort of punishment. The bony skull of the pachycephalosaurid would appear to have the same adaptations. The bony structure seemed to radiate into the dome giving a strength that would withstand a head butting. The backbone also appears to have been stiffened to absorb the impact after a headlong charge.

However, recent researches seem to refute this evocative image. The geometry seems wrong for one thing. A bulbous dome hitting a bulbous dome would have to do so with a spot-on accuracy, or else they would bounce off sideways and have no effect. Perhaps, then, they head-butted each other's flanks?

Now, however, it seems that this strong radiating impact resistant structure was only present in juveniles, and had disappeared once the animals were adults—the time when head butting would have been employed. It looks as if the heads of the adults were covered in some kind of horny case, maybe producing a spectacular ornamentation that we can only guess at.

**Left and below:** *If a bonehead used its tough skull as a battering ram, its heavy head would have been balanced by its stiffened tail. A fight between boneheads may have been only one of intimidation and display, without much damage being done to their combatant.*

# Scelidosaurus

Back in the early days of dinosaur development the two-footed ornithischians gave rise to another major stream of the dinosaur dynasty. *Scutellosaurus* was close to the ancestry of this. The array of armor along its back was an early indication of what direction this line was taking. What subsequently developed was a group that came to be known as the thyreophorans—the dinosaurs with armor.

Two major groups of the thyreophorans are known—the stegosaurids that were important in late Jurassic and early Cretaceous times, and the ankylosaurids that took over in the late Cretaceous. In the 1980s that the two groups were united under the banner of the thyreophorans, before that the received opinion was that they had come from separate ancestors and had developed their armor independently. The early history is rather vague, the lack of early Jurassic specimens leading to the belated updating of the classification. The only exception was one dinosaur discovered in the lower Jurassic rocks of southern England in 1858, and this was *Scelidosaurus*.

## A FINE EARLY FIND

*Scelidosaurus* was really the first fully articulated dinosaur skeleton to come to light. Unfortunately it was at the time when the full nature of dinosaurs was not well appreciated, and the science was obscured

*Scelidosaurus was one of the earliest armored dinosaurs. Its remains were found in Lower Jurassic rocks.*

by scientific rivalry. The description published by Sir Richard Owen in 1861 did not do the fossil justice, and despite the fact that the skeleton was almost complete, *Scelidosaurus* did not seize the public's imagination as *Iguanodon* or *Megalosaurus* did.

In *Scelidosaurus* we have a heavy animal, about 13 feet (4 meters) long. The front legs are a little shorter than the hind, but not to the extent of most other dinosaurs. This in itself suggests that it was a four-footed animal. It is surprising that Owen did not pick up on this, as it would have helped to underpin his hypothesis that *Iguanodon* and *Megalosaurus*, the other two dinosaurs known at that time, were big four-footed animals. A primitive aspect of the hipbone was the

**Left**: *The foot bones (shown here, from two different specimens) and the hand bones of* Scelidosaurus *indicate that they were built to take the weight of the animal by spreading the weight evenly between the toes.* Scelidosaurus *was therefore a four-footed beast.*

lack of the prepubic process—that part of the swept-back pubis that protruded forward and sideways. It was present in the stegosaurids and the ankylosaurids, but had not developed in *Scelidosaurus*. Its feet were quite long and had toes with hoof-like claws. The toes could open quite wide to spread the weight of the big body. The tail was long and heavy and could have been used as a balance if *Scelidosaurus* had raised itself on its hind legs and put on a short burst of speed or to reach overhanging vegetation. However, speed was not the method used to save this animal from harm so it must have relied on its armor.

## EARLY ARMOR

The armor consisted of bony plates forming a broad covering across its back and sides. Clusters of bony knobs graced the corners of the skull. The bony plates were undoubtedly the bases of horny spikes that stuck out along the sides and the back. A newer specimen actually has traces of the

230   220   210   200   190   180   170   160   15

TRIASSIC                    JURASSIC

 SCELIDOSAURUS

EMAUSAURUS

LUSITANOSAURUS

## FACTFILE

**The first bones to be described as *Scelidosaurus* were found before the discovery of the almost-complete skeleton. These are now known to have belonged to something else. By the rules of nomenclature it should have been given a different name, but, in this case, the regulations have been waived.**

themselves in trying to make the scientific name of a new dinosaur significant. In this instance the name is an acronym of the name of the university where it was studied—Ernst-Mopritz-Arndt-Universität. It was discovered in Lower Jurassic rocks in Germany in 1990 and although its remains are fragmentary, it seems to have been very similar to *Scelidosaurus* in its size and its armor of bony plates. However, it was only about half the length.

skin, and these show a mosaic of small, rounded scales embedded in the skin surface.

Another dinosaur, *Lusitanosaurus*, lived in the early Jurassic of Portugal. Only a jawbone fragment with teeth are known, but these look very similar to those of *Scelidosaurus*. They are, however, different enough to show that they belong to a different animal.

Yet another was *Emausaurus*. Sometimes paleontologists excel

### SCELIDOSAURUS LIFESTYLE

The teeth of *Scelidosaurus* are leaf-shaped and coarsely serrated along the upper edges. It looks as if it crushed its food with a pestle-and-mortar action—the upper tooth being the pestle and the lower tooth row the mortar. This is quite different from the grinding action of the ornithopods or the chopping action of the ceratopsians.

The skeleton of *Scelidosaurus* was

| 140 | 130 | 120 | 110 | 100 | 90 | 80 | 70 | 60 |
|-----|-----|-----|-----|-----|-----|-----|-----|-----|

CRETACEOUS

found in marine beds, lying upside down. This led to early speculations that it may have been a sea-living animal. Now the preferred scenario is that it lived well inland, and when it died its body was washed down rivers to the sea. In the process of its decay it insides filled with gas, buoying up the corpse for some time. Like this the animal would have floated on its back, the heavy armor acting as a keel. Eventually, when the body cavity ruptured, the gases escaped and the corpse sank, it would have settled on the seabed belly up. Many ankylos-aurids are found like this, leading to speculation that these animals habited upland areas drained by rivers.

So why was the armor developed? Defense is the obvious answer, but against what? It was before the time of the really big theropods, but medium-sized theropods existed then. The trouble is that no actual remains have been found in the rocks of that area and that period. The circumstances of its fossilization make it appear that *Scelidosaurus* was alone.

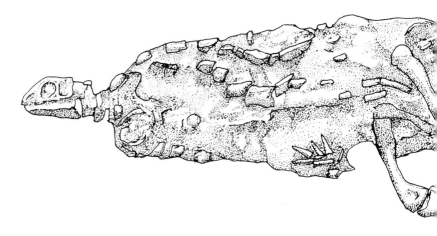

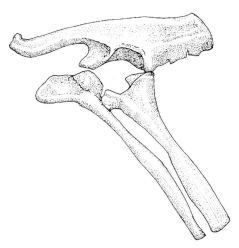

**Left**: *The hip bones are typical of an ornithischian, with the pubis bone lying back against the ischium.*

**Below**: *The skeleton of Scelidosaurus was one of the first almost complete dinosaur skeletons to be found—in 1863. It was over a century before any serious attempt was made to extract it from the block of limestone in which it was embedded.*

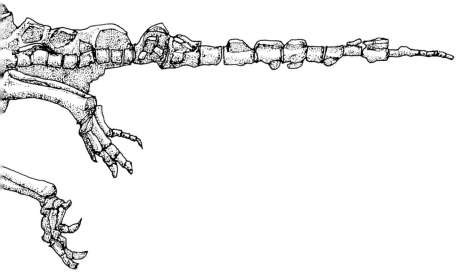

# Stegosaurus

*S*tegosaurus is unmistakable anywhere; the double row of vertical plates along its neck and back flashing in the sun, the powerful tail with its wicked spines swinging languorously from side to side, the shoulders swaggering back and forth giving its short front legs the reach to enable them to keep pace with the plod of its hind feet, and the tiny head with its little eyes peering stupidly this way and that.

We are back on the Morrison Formation plains of late Jurassic North America and keeping the company of one of the most recognizable dinosaurs.

## PLATED REPTILE

*Stegosaurus* is the best known of the stegosaurid group. It is the biggest as well. Although many nearly complete skeletons are known, there are still many questions to be answered about this spectacular beast. We know that the plates were arranged in a double row down the backbone, but just how were they placed? As there is no direct connection between the plates and the backbone—they are merely embedded in the skin and flesh—there is some uncertainty as to how they were arranged in life. Perhaps they were arranged in pairs. Perhaps they were arranged in a double row alternating. Perhaps they were arranged in a single row but slightly

overlapping to give an alternating effect. There have even been arguments for the plates lying flat against the flanks, or even sticking out sideways at right angles. The general consensus at present is that they were placed in an alternating double row.

*The stegosaurs were the plated dinosaurs of the late Jurassic and early Cretaceous. The biggest and most famous was* Stegosaurus *(left) from North America. Others included* Tuojiangosaurus *(below) from China and* Kentrosaurus *(bottom) from Africa.*

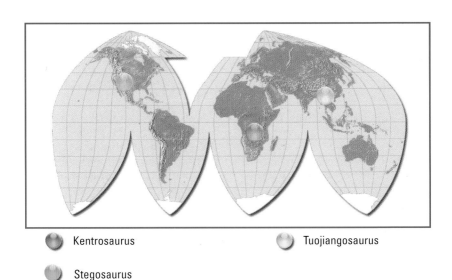

⬤ Kentrosaurus ⬤ Tuojiangosaurus

⬤ Stegosaurus

To decide on the arrangement of the plates we must first look at their function. What were they used for? There are two schools of thought on this. The first is that they were a defensive measure, and the second that they were a heat exchange mechanism.

**DIFFERING IDEAS**

As a defensive measure they would have been covered in horn, probably drawn out into wicked points and with

230 220 210 200 190 180 170 160 15

TRIASSIC JURASSIC

cuttingly sharp edges. There is no direct evidence for this. All we have are the fossils of the plates of bone that form the cores. If this were the case the plates in life would have been maybe twice the area as presented by the naked bone. Many paleontologists are worried about their arrangement. Horny plates sticking up in the air would not offer a great deal of protection, even for the backbone that would be the nearest part of the skeleton. It was this assumption that led to the idea that the plates may have lain flat on the flanks or have been sticking out sideways. Bob Bakker, in the 1980s suggested that the bases of the plates were embedded in powerful muscles and could be turned and pointed towards any attacker.

As a heat exchange mechanism the plates would have been covered in skin, and so the plates would not have been very much larger than the area presented by the bone. The skin would have been full of blood vessels, in a perfect position to absorb the heat of the sun in the early morning, or to expel waste heat into the wind during the heat of the day. An alternating arrangement of plates would be ideal for this, allowing air to circulate to them all and allowing sunlight to fall on the maximum area. Possible evidence is the presence of channels in the bone of the plate that must have carried blood vessels. However, horny sheaths would have needed blood vessels as well.

Whichever, if they were covered in horn or covered in skin, they would probably have been brightly colored, and used for signaling to one another—display devices.

Whether armor or heat-regulator, they would have needed some kind of organizational control. This brings us to the next quandary—the size of the head. For an animal as big as a car the head was tiny, and it contained the smallest brain of any dinosaur in relation to the

| 140 | 130 | 120 | 110 | 100 | 90 | 80 | 70 | 60 |
|---|---|---|---|---|---|---|---|---|

CRETACEOUS

STEGOSAURUS
HESPEROSAURUS
TUOJIANGOSAURUS
YINGASHANOSAURUS
KENTROSAURUS

WUERHOSAURUS

size of its body. This led to an old idea that it must have had an auxiliary brain somewhere else. That somewhere else was in the hips, where a cavity existed in the region of the spinal cord. Perhaps this was the site of a second brain that controlled the hind legs and the tail? Modern science says no. There was a gap there certainly, but it probably contained a gland to help control the energy used by the hindquarters.

There was certainly armor on the body of *Stegosaurus*. The first skeletons were found with little tubercles and medallions of bone associated

with them. It was assumed that these had been embedded in the skin in a random pattern all over the body. It now seems likely that they formed a kind of a flexible mail cover for the throat. At the other end of the animal there were two pairs of spikes towards the tip of the tail. These pointed sideways and would have been used as a weapon, swung with some force against the legs and flanks of any attacking theropod dinosaur.

## THE STEGOSAURID CLAN

An argument against the plates being a heat exchange mechanism is that none of the other

**Above:** *The skeleton of* Stegosaurus *shows a four-footed animal with a double row of plates down its back. The head is tiny and the front legs are much smaller than the rear. The tail is armed with spikes for defense.*

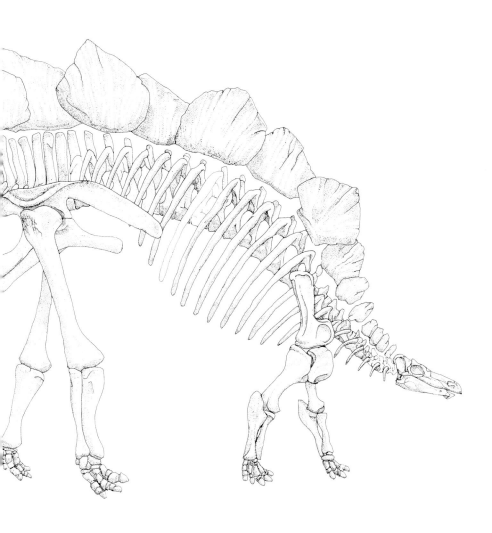

stegosaurids possessed plates of a sufficient area. *Hesperosaurus*, which was like a smaller more primitive version of *Stegosaurus* and also from the Morrison Formation, had big plates, but the others did not. Mostly they had very much narrower plates.

*Wuerhosaurus,* from early Cretaceous China, was a big one too—about the same size as *Stegosaurus*. However, its plates seem to have been long and low.

*Tuojiangosaurus*, from the late Jurassic of China, had narrow triangular plates. Many of the stegosaurid finds have been in China.

*Kentrosaurus*, one of the Tendaguru fauna uncovered by a German expedition in East Africa in the early years of the twentieth century, had plates that were very narrow and only went as far as the hips. The tail spines ran down the length of the tail. Another feature of *Kentrosaurus* was a pair of sideways-pointing spikes that guarded the shoulders or the hips. Most of the other stegosaurids possessed these as well.

The shoulder spines on

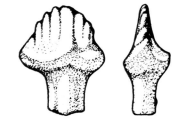

*Yingashanosaurus* were truly enormous, sticking out of the side of the animal like a pair of angel's wings.

Stegosaurids were a big part of the scene in late Jurassic and early Cretaceous times. Until recently the only late Cretaceous example was *Dravidosaurus* from India. This was put down to the fact that in late Cretaceous times India was an island continent not long separated from what was left of Pangaea. As an island it would have had its own interpretation of the rules of evolution, and there would have been dinosaurs living on insular India that did not exist anywhere else on earth—like the marsupials of modern Australia.

Perhaps India was the refuge of groups of dinosaurs that were elsewhere extinct. A fine theory, but the fossil of *Dravidosaurus*, which was thought to have been a stegosaurid, turned out to have been nothing more than the misidentified remains of a plesiosaur—a contemporary sea reptile. So, no stegosaurids are known from the late Cretaceous. The late Cretaceous was the time of a different group of armor bearers altogether.

**Left**: *The tiny skull of the* Stegosaurus *(left) had a beak at the front of the mouth and very small leaf-shaped teeth (top, left) for chopping plants.*

**Right**: *The hands (top, right) and the feet (bottom, right) of* Stegosaurus, *with short toes and stout hooves, were adapted for carrying the great weight of the animal.*

# Primitive Ankylosaurs and Nodosaurids

The armored dinosaurs of the late Cretaceous were quite different from those of the late Jurassic. These were the ankylosaurs, and where the stegosaurids went for height with their flamboyant upward flowing plates, the ankylosaurs tended to go for width.

Two main groups are acknowledged, the nodosaurids and the ankylosaurids, with a minor early group, the polacanthids.

### EARLY DISCOVERIES

*Hylaeosaurus* was, along with its early cousin *Scelidosaurus*, one of the first dinosaurs to have been discovered. It was found in early Cretaceous rocks southern England in 1833 by Gideon Mantell, of *Iguanodon* fame. It was only a partial skeleton and there little to show what the full animal looked like. Since then there have been no more remains of this beast found and we are no wiser. However, some paleontologists think that it may be the same animal as *Polacanthus*, found thirty years later on the nearby Isle of Wight. The problem is that, although we only know the forequarters of *Hylaeosaurus*, we only know the hindquarters of

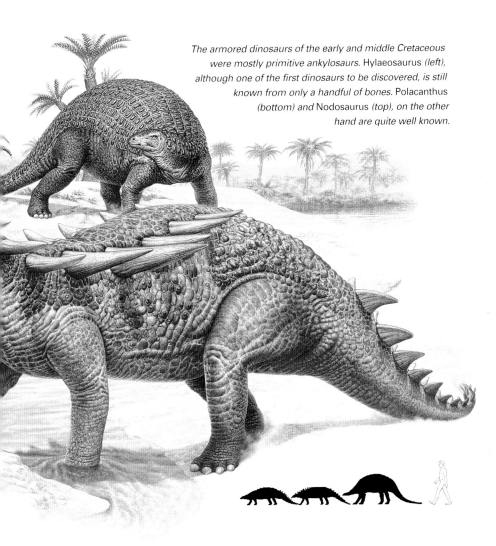

The armored dinosaurs of the early and middle Cretaceous were mostly primitive ankylosaurs. Hylaeosaurus *(left)*, although one of the first dinosaurs to be discovered, is still known from only a handful of bones. Polacanthus *(bottom)* and Nodosaurus *(top)*, on the other hand are quite well known.

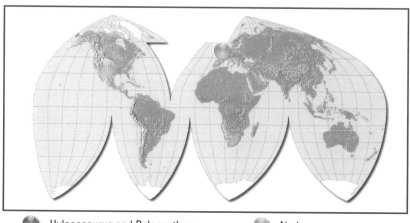

 Hylaeosaurus and Polacanthus      Nodosaurus

*Polacanthus*. Current thinking is that the two animals are distinct genera, largely because *Hyalaeosaurus* comes from slightly earlier rocks, and the types of armor differ in detail between the two.

*Polacanthus* was a primitive member of the ankylosaurs. It may have been more closely related to the ankylosaurids than the nodosaurids. The armor was of three different types. Over the body was a series of spikes that stock upwards or sideways, or both. The tail was flanked by rows of triangular plates that protruded sideways. These were probably the bases of sharp horny spikes, like

| 230 | 220 | 210 | 200 | 190 | 180 | 170 | 160 | 15( |
|-----|-----|-----|-----|-----|-----|-----|-----|-----|

**TRIASSIC**           **JURASSIC**

MYMOORAPELTA

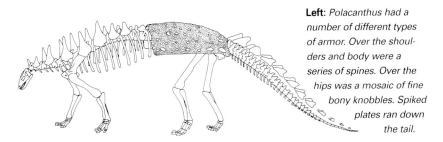

**Left:** *Polacanthus had a number of different types of armor. Over the shoulders and body were a series of spines. Over the hips was a mosaic of fine bony knobbles. Spiked plates ran down the tail.*

those proposed for *Stegosaurus*. The tail would have been a weapon that could have been swung from side to side to combat an attack. The strangest piece of armor was over the hips. It was a solid mass of fused bony lumps forming a shield. For a time it was thought that this was just the way the armor had fossilized, but now we know of closely related animals for North America, *Gastonia* and *Mymoorapelta*, that had exactly the same feature. It appears that this sacral buckler was a genuine feature of *Polacanthus* and its relatives.

## NODOSAURIDS

The nodosaurids proper arrived on the scene somewhat later. They continued the tradition of *Polacanthus* in having spiky armor over the forequarters. The bulk of the armor consisted of a tight mosaic of tiny bony ossicles covering the whole of the upper surface of the animal. The pelvis was truly massive, with the ilium bone overhanging the legs, and used as an anchor for the enormous muscles needed to support such a heavy animal. The pubis and ischium bones, on the other hand, were tiny.

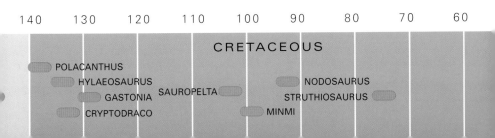

| 140 | 130 | 120 | 110 | 100 | 90 | 80 | 70 | 60 |
|---|---|---|---|---|---|---|---|---|

### CRETACEOUS

POLACANTHUS

HYLAEOSAURUS

GASTONIA    SAUROPELTA

CRYPTODRACO

MINMI

NODOSAURUS

STRUTHIOSAURUS

The nodosasurid skull was very narrow and the natural set of the neck brought the muzzle close to the ground. This probably sheds some light on the feeding habits of these animals. They probably grazed the low-growing vegetation of the time, and the narrow snout suggests that they were quite selective about what they ate. As flowering plants evolved in late Cretaceous times it is tempting to visualize the massive nodosaurids nibbling on buttercups and the other herbaceous flowers that thrived then.

*Sauropelta* was one of the earliest. It seems to have been very abundant on the early Cretaceous plains of North America. Footprints, given the ichnogenus *Tetrapodosaurus*, were probably made by these beasts.

*Nodosaurus* itself has always been regarded as the typical nodosaurid. However its appearance is still not fully understood. It probably had the side spikes that seem to be common to them all, but it is often restored without.

An early Cretaceous nodosaurid has even been found in Australia. Sheep-sized *Minmi* has the distinction of having the shortest name in the dinosaur lexicon.

The bones of nodosaurids are quite

---

## FACTFILE

A cololite—the fossilized remains of stomach contents—has been found inside the skeleton of *Minmi*, the Australian nodosaurid. It contains the remains of fruiting bodies of flowering plants. It seems likely that these dinosaurs played an important part in the dispersal of the plant seeds of the time.

---

distinctive. When they are discovered in isolation it is usually quite evident that it is a nodosaurid bone discovered. So many nodosaurid genera have been set up on the basis of very fragmentary material. *Cryptodraco* ("hidden dragon") from the late Jurassic of England even has a name that acknowledges this.

### A DWARF

In appearance *Struthiosaurus* would have looked just like any other of the nodosaurid group, with its mosaic of back armor, its spines around the shoulders, and its sideways pointing spikes on the tail. However, it was only about the size of a sheep. It was found in Upper Cretaceous rocks of Romania, and also from France, Hungary, and

Austria. Small duckbill dinosaurs are also found in these areas. The reason is that in late Cretaceous times the region of southern Europe was on the northern edge if the Tethys ocean—a vast seaway that separated the northern continents from Africa and the rest of Gondwana. The Tethys has been closing ever since and all that is left of it nowadays is the Mediterranean and the drying puddles of the Black, Caspian, and Aral Seas. In late Cretaceous times it was still quite wide and the northern

continent had strings of islands off its shores. The dwarf dinosaurs probably lived on these islands. Dwarfism is a common evolutionary response to the limited food supplies on islands—a smaller animal needing less to eat. In Tertiary times there were elephants the size of pigs on Mediterranean islands, and the modern equivalents are the dwarf hippopotamus from Madagascar and the little Shetland pony of the Scottish Hebrides. This principle seems to have worked in dinosaur times too.

**Left**: *The ankylosaurs that had the armor that stuck out at the side could probably have hunkered down on the ground when danger approached. In such a position it would have been difficult for a meat-eater to turn it over.*

# Ankylosaurids

**M**ore familiar than the nodosaurids in the popular psyche are the ankylosaurids. These were the armored thyreophorans with the club at the end of the tail.

The biggest of these was *Ankylosaurus* itself, from the late Cretaceous of North America. Unfortunately we do not know a great deal about it. We only know of fragmentary specimens, probably because it lived on uplands far away from any good place for animals to be buried and fossilized. The remains that we do have would probably have been washed down rivers to the sea. What we do know was that it must have been something like 25 feet (7.5 meters) long. It was one of the last of the dinosaurs to have existed.

## ANKYLOSAURID HEAD

To see what an ankylosaurid looked like, it is best to study a better-known example, *Euoplocephalus* is an early relative of *Ankylosaurus*.

Starting at the front, the head was very much broader than that of a nodosaurid, sometimes as broad as it was long. The head was a solid mass of bone, the individual struts and slabs of bone making up the usual dinosaur skull having been fused together so that the joins cannot be seen. Usually a dinosaur skull is full of gaps and holes. In an ankylosaur these are all gone—only the eye sockets and the nostrils remaining. The surface of the skull

*The big armored dinosaurs, such as* Euoplocephalus *(below) and* Pinacosaurus *(right) at the end of the Cretaceous had bony clubs at the end of the tail. They are known from North America and from China.*

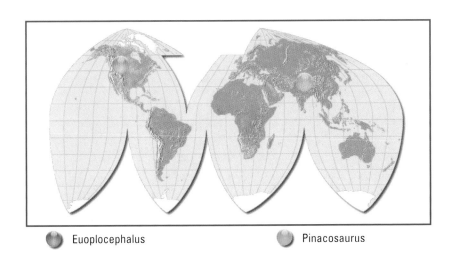

🔵 Euoplocephalus      🔵 Pinacosaurus

was a rigid mass of bony plates that, in life, would have had horny coverings. A strongly armored head indeed. In fact even the eyelids were armored. Curved plates of bone inside the eye sockets would have slammed shut like the steel shutters of a battleship whenever any danger approached. Inside the skull

was a labyrinth of air passages—the nodosaurids had these too. Air would have circulated here, passing over damp membranes, and helped to cool off the brain during hot weather. A feature not often found in dinosaurs was a palate, a shelf of bone that separated the nasal chambers from the

230     220     210     200     190     180     170     160     15

TRIASSIC                       JURASSIC

mouth. This would have meant that an ankyloasurid would have been able to eat and breathe at the same time.

The broad beak and jaws would mean that it would have been a much less fussy eater than a nodosaurid, just cropping off the undergrowth indiscriminately as it walked along. The teeth were small and fluted. They have been described as being like little hands with the fingers together. There must have been a big muscular tongue, judging by the bones around the back of the mouth where the tongue muscles would have been anchored. The gap for the cheeks was much deeper than that of other ornithischian dinosaurs. It looks as if it cropped great mouthfuls of undergrowth and chopped it up in the mouth, holding it in the cheeks and circulating it with the tongue. There may have been fermenting vats, like a cow's stomach, in the body, in which bacterial action helped to break down the cellulose in the plant material—the body volume was certainly big enough for this. Some skeletons, but not all, also contain stomach stones. Stomach contents have been found inside an ankylosaur skeleton that show bits of plant stems as well as seeds and fern spores. Not only does this show what it had been eating before its death, but also how it had been eating. The plant stems had been snipped of as if by a beak or scissor-like teeth, but had not been ground up as they would have been if the teeth had been used for grinding.

## THE ARMOR

The armor of an ankylosaurid was basically the same as that of a nodosaurid—a groundmass of little tubercles with bigger keeled plates embedded in it. The shoulder spines that were present were not the spectacular sideways-pointing spikes of the nodosaurids, but more modest upward-pointing structures. Heavy

| 140 | 130 | 120 | 110 | 100 | 90 | 80 | 70 | 60 |
|-----|-----|-----|-----|-----|----|----|----|-----|

CRETACEOUS

ANKYLOSAURUS

EUOPLOCEPHALUS

PINACOSAURUS

rectangular plates formed broad bands across the neck and shoulders.

It had the same deep body and similar broad hips with flaring ischium bone and reduced pubis and ischium.

The sides of the backbone were reinforced with bony tendons as a help to support the animal's great weight. The tendons became thicker and sturdier in the tail and in the last half of the tail they helped to fuse the vertebrae into an inflexible shaft. This was actually the handle of a club. At the very end of the tail bones embedded in the skin became big and solid, forming heavy lobes at each side, probably covered in horn. These formed the famous club of the ankylosaurids.

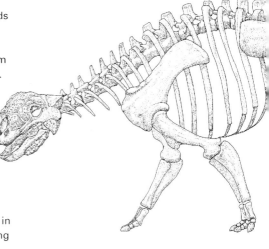

The nodosaurids and the ankylosaurids had markedly different modes of defense. The armor of the nodosaurids seems to have been heavier than that of the ankylosaurids, suggesting that their defense was more passive. The position of the limb muscles seems to indicate that they could fold their legs beneath them and hunker down close to the ground. This would have made it difficult for any big predator, such as a *Tyrannosaurus*, to turn the animal over and reach its

## FACTFILE

The tail club evolved again relatively recently, but amongst the mammals. *Doedicurus* was a glyptodont—a kind of a giant armadillo—from the Ice Age. As well as having a back and tail covered in armor, it had a spiky club at the tail end, evidently used exactly the same way as the ankylosaurids used theirs.

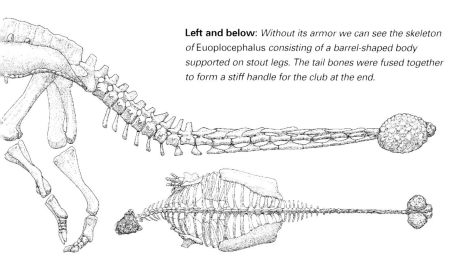

**Left and below**: *Without its armor we can see the skeleton of* Euoplocephalus *consisting of a barrel-shaped body supported on stout legs. The tail bones were fused together to form a stiff handle for the club at the end.*

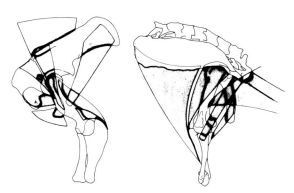

**Left**: *The arm (far left) and leg muscles (left) of a big ankylosaur were huge. They would have to have been, to support the great weight of armor.*

vulnerable and unprotected belly. Some paleontologists, though, think this is unlikely. To make this form of defense effective, the spines would have to have been bigger in the hip area rather than the shoulder. They think the mode of defense was more active. The weapons of a nodosaurid were the spines that stuck sideways from the shoulders. These animals would have charged their enemies head on, lunging at them with their spines. They would also have been able to swing their tails at them, the sideways pointing plates of the tail

acting like axe blades. The sideways spines of the shoulders would also have had another function. Like the horns of the ceratopsians and the antlers of modern deer, they were probably used for ritual combat, when males were sparring with one another for the privilege of mating with the females of the herd. Rather than damage one another permanently they could have locked shoulder spines and pushed and pulled until the weaker gave up and retired.

The ankylosaurids, on the other hand, have always been shown to be much more active in their defense. They would have used their tails. The heavy club, when swung with all the force of the muscles at the hips, and given leverage by the stiffness of the bony tendons, would smash into the legs of an attacking theropod and inflict serious damage. It has also been suggested that the coloring may have

been a factor in defense. There may have been an eyespot on the tail—essentially a fake eye. This would have given the club on the end of the tail the appearance of a sauropod head on the end of a long neck. A *Tyrannosaurus* acting on instinct would have gone for the supposed head and found that it was biting on a solid mass of bone. This is totally speculative, but it is an interesting idea. There are several *Tyrannosaurus* remains in which the leg bones are damaged—just the sort of damage that would be caused by an ankylosaurid club. There is no evidence of damage to *Tyrannosaurus* skulls that would result if the predator attacked a tail club by mistake.

*Ankylosaurus* and *Euoplocephalus* are probably the best known of the ankylosaurids. They are both North American examples. Most others come from Asia.

**Left**: *The ankylosaurids protected themselves by giving meat-eating dinosaurs a mighty slap with their massive tail clubs. A well-aimed blow could easily have killed a predatory dinosaur.*

# The First Pterosaurs

Dinosaurs were not the only inhabitants of the world during the age of reptiles. They shared the Mesozoic world with all sorts of other animals. While the dinosaurs were the most important animals on land, it was their cousins, the pterosaurs that ruled the skies.

Pterosaurs are familiar to us all, usually under the popular term "pterodactyls." They took the place of the birds in the Mesozoic skies, and existed until long after the birds evolved. Like birds they ranged in size. Most were quite small but some were the size of small aircraft. They all had leathery wings, supported on an elongated finger. Some had long tails, some did not. Their different heads and arrangement of jaws and teeth, reflected their different lifestyles.

There were two main evolutionary lines of pterosaurs. First the rhamphorhychoids, who came into being at about the same time as the dinosaurs in the late Triassic, and then the pterodactyloids, who took over in the late Jurassic. The pterodactyloids coexisted with the rhamphorhychoids for a time, and thrived until the end of the Cretaceous when they met the same fate as the dinosaurs.

**Below:** *The ancestors of both the dinosaurs and the pterosaurs are to be found amongst the two-footed thecodonts of the Triassic.* Heleosaurus *would have been a typical candidate.*

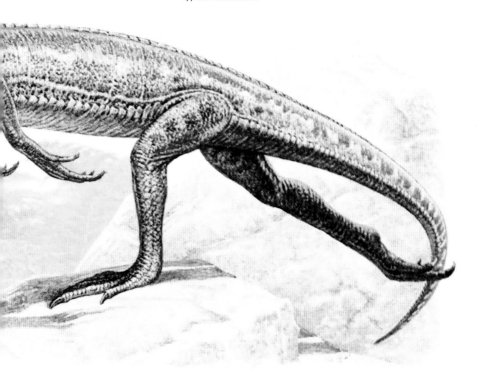

# Early Rhamphorhynchoids

The renowned fossil collector Mary Anning discovered a pterosaur in the lower Jurassic rocks of southern England in 1828. For a long time it was believed that the early Jurassic was the time of the first pterosaurs. Then, in the 1880s, a skeleton with long finger-like bones was discovered in upper Triassic rocks in Italy and was originally regarded as a pterosaur. When it turned out to be a totally different reptile altogether, and the long bones were from a particularly long neck, the idea of Triassic pterosaurs was disregarded for a century. But then, in the 1970s, true Triassic pterosaurs began to turn up in southern Europe.

*Prenodactylus* was a typical early rhamphorhynchoid. It was found in 1978 in Triassic limestones in northern Italy. It was about the size of a jay and the leathery wings were supported on long finger bones that were about as thick as the bones of the arm. The neck was quite short and the head jaws were long. It had sharp teeth of different sizes. The tail was very long and inflexible and the vertebrae were lashed together with tendons. At the end there was probably a diamond-shaped vane, used for steering. It was a warm-blooded animal and so it would have been covered in fur. These last features—the vane on the tail and the covering of fur—are conjectural, but based on what we know of other pterosaurs it seems

Preondactylus *from the Triassic, was one of the earliest of the pterosaurs. Even at this early stage the typical pterosaur features were present.*

likely that they were present.

Another early rhamphorhynchoid was *Eudimorphodon*. This was actually the earliest pterosaur known. The teeth were very odd for such an early animal—we would have expected something very primitive. Instead we see two types of teeth—a bunch of long sharp fangs at the front and a row of smaller, multi-cusped teeth behind. There are two extra pairs of fangs in the upper jaw about half way along. The only interpretation of dentition like this is that the animal was a fish-catcher. The long fangs would have been used for snatching the fish from the water as it flew low, and the smaller multi-cusped teeth would have been able to crush the scaly body once the fish had been caught. In fact, the scales of fish are found associated with the fossil of *Eudimorphodon* that was also found in the Triassic rocks of Italy.

## DANGEROUS SEAS

The pterosaurs did not have it all their own way when it came to fish. We know of a specimen of *Prenodactylus* that was found in a coprolite—a fossilized lump of dung. It appears as if the pterosaur was eaten by a big fish, and the indigestible bones passed

*The Triassic pterosaurs, such as Peteinosaurus (below) and Eudimorphodon (top right), all belonged to the rhamphorhynchoid family. They had narrow wings, short wrist bones and long tails with a rudder on the end.*

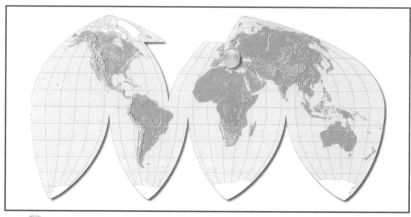

Eudimorphodon and Peteinosaurus

through the fish's digestive system, later to be fossilized in a tangled lump left on the sea bed.

The sea in which these pterosaurs fished, and occasionally met their end, was the Tethys Ocean—a vast stretch of water that separated the northern continents from the southern. At this time all the continents were one mass—the supercontinent Pangaea— but the Tethys took the form of a great embayment that reached in from the east, almost splitting the super- continent in half. The pterosaurs would have inhabited the shallow shoreline, and were fossilized in the limestones

| 230 | 220 | 210 | 200 | 190 | 180 | 170 | 160 | 15 |
|---|---|---|---|---|---|---|---|---|

TRIASSIC                                    JURASSIC

PREONDACTYLUS
EUDIMORPHODON
PETEINOSAURUS

that were laid down there.

Many pterosaurs are found without their heads. The interpretation is that when they died and fell into the sea they were light enough to float about while they decomposed. The head was always the heaviest part of the corpse, and it eventually fell off and sank away while the rest of the body floated for some time before sinking.

*Peteinosaurus* also lived at the same time and the same place as *Eudimorphodon*. It was a little smaller, about the size of a pigeon as opposed to the size of a crow. Its teeth were very much more primitive—all the same size and shape. It seems likely that *Eudimorphodon* was an insect-eater rather than a fish-eater. Already the pterosaur group was diversifying into different lifestyles and niches. The primitive nature of the teeth suggest that this animal was very close to the ancestral line that led to the rest of the rhamphorhynchoid group.

## FACTFILE

In 2004 the first pterosaur eggs were discovered in Argentina. They showed that pterosaurs laid eggs with leathery shells, like modern reptiles, rather than with hard shells, like dinosaurs and modern birds.

### AN EARLY PTEROSAUR FIND

Anyway, all of this was of no interest to fossil collector Mary Anning when she found the bones of *Dimorphodon* in the lower Jurassic rocks of southern England in 1828. She was one of the first professional fossil collectors, more famous for her discoveries of the great sea reptiles of the Jurassic than for pterosaur remains. She provided the scientists of the day with their raw material. Her pterosaur specimen was studied and described by William

| 140 | 130 | 120 | 110 | 100 | 90 | 80 | 70 | 60 |
|---|---|---|---|---|---|---|---|---|

CRETACEOUS

**Below**: *The skeleton of* Eudimorphodon *was similar to that of
all rhamphorhynchoids. The
different members of the group
differed from one another
usually in the shape of the skull
and the arrangement of teeth.*

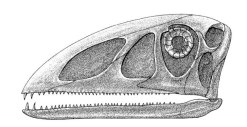

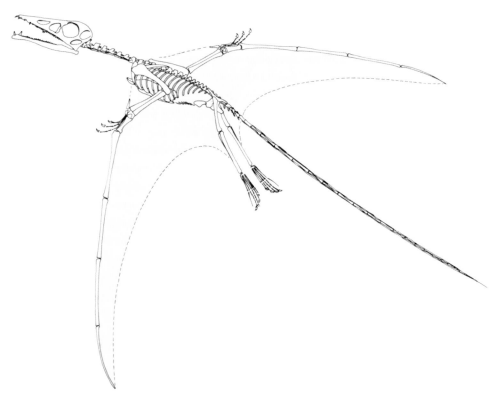

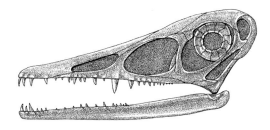

**Left**: *The skull of* Peteinosaurus *was deep and narrow and had many small cusped teeth.*

**Right**: Preondactylus *had a skull with narrow jaws containing a variety of sizes of teeth.*

Buckland, of *Megalosaurus* fame, who realized it was the remains of a flying reptile, like those that were being discovered in Germany at the time. It was not until 1858 that the skull of this animal was found, and it was studied and described by Sir Richard Owen. It was he who gave it the name *Dimorphodon* "two shapes of teeth" after the arrangement of teeth in the mouth.

The skull of this pterosaur was short and high. It had enormous openings that reduced the structure of the skull to a lightweight framework of bone. It had four large front teeth in each side of the upper jaw, followed by many smaller pointed teeth. In the lower jaw the big teeth at the front were followed by rows of even smaller teeth. This arrangement has been interpreted as the dentition of a fish-eater. The big

area presented by the side of the head may well have been brightly colored, like a puffin's bill, and used for signaling and display. The eye socket has a sclerotic ring—a ring made up of little bones. This may have protected the eye against the buffeting of the wind or may have helped in focusing on prey.

The legs were quite long for a pterosaur, and the finger and toe claws were quite big, suggesting that *Dimorphodon* was a good climber and rested on tree trunks or cliff faces. The wings were quite short for the size of animal, probably better adapted for tight maneuvering than sustained soaring, judging from the morphology of present day birds. Only a few remains of *Dimorphodon* have been found, and these have all been from southern England.

# Primitive Rhamphorhynchoids

As the Jurassic developed, so did the rhamphorhynchoids. But where did they come from initially?

The pterosaurs in general were closely related to the dinosaurs, about as closely related as crocodiles were. The ancestors of these—pterosaurs, dinosaurs, and crocodiles—would have been found in among primitive lizard-like examples of the archosaur group. They would have been very active animals, scampering about and feeding on insects. At an early stage they would have been able to rise to their hind legs and take to running. How and why the wings evolved is still a mystery. They may have taken to a tree-living lifestyle and developed a gliding membrane to allow them long jumps from branch to branch, rather like the flying squirrels of today. Selective pressures would have ensured that a more controllable surface evolved to make these leaps more efficient and then the wings proper would have developed. This is all speculation, of course. There are no

Dimorphodon *was one of the first of the pterosaurs to have been studied scientifically. We know of most of the skeleton, but none of the soft anatomy has ever been discovered.*

Fine lake deposits in Kazakhstan have produced the detailed remains of several pterosaurs. The most interesting are the rhamphorhynchoids Sordes *(left and top right)*, that had its hairy pelt preserved, and Batrachognathus *(right)*, with its broad frog-like mouth.

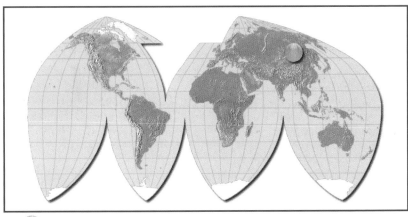

Sordes and Batrachognathus

fossils that show such early stages of the wing development. The fossil record is short of transitional forms like this.

### FURRY FIND

We mentioned earlier that the pterosaurs were warm-blooded and covered in hair for insulation. The hair covering was pure speculation until the 1970s. Then the skeleton of *Sordes* was found in lake deposits in upper Jurassic rocks in Kazakhstan, in the western foothills of the Tien-shan. It was a small, starling-sized pterosaur with long jaws and sharp teeth. The most remarkable thing about it, though, was

| 230 | 220 | 210 | 200 | 190 | 180 | 170 | 160 | 15 |

TRIASSIC                                    JURASSIC

DIMORPHODON

the covering of fine fur that could be seen in the rocks around the skeleton. The sediments were formed at the bottom of an inland lake, where there were few currents and little to disturb the water. The deposits were so fine that they could preserve the traces of very fine structures. Insect fossils are abundant here, and they show a great resemblance to insect fossils from fine late Jurassic deposits in other parts of the world. Some scientists dismissed the fur covering in this little pterosaur as a mineral growth deposited by ground water, and indeed fossils sometimes do show such a growth. However, closer inspection showed that this was really a furry coat. Over the body the hair reached lengths of about a $\frac{1}{5}$ inch (6 millimeters) and it was also found, but more sparsely, on the flight membrane, the skin between the toes and the base of the tail. The rest of the tail was bare. It is now

## FACTFILE

**The fourth finger of a pterosaur was the one that supported the wing. It consisted of four sturdy bones, the biggest of which were longer and thicker than the bones of the arm. The three fingers that comprise the hand seem ridiculously small in comparison.**

assumed that all pterosaurs had such a hair covering.

### VARIED DIETS

The jaws of *Sordes* were typical of a rhamphorhynchoid—long and narrow and full of little sharp teeth. Those of its contemporary in the area, *Batrachognathus*, however, were quite different. They were broad and rounded, and rather like those of a frog—hence the name, which means

| 140 | 130 | 120 | 110 | 100 | 90 | 80 | 70 | 60 |

CRETACEOUS

BATRACHOGNATHUS

SORDES

"frog jaw." The rounded jaws were set with stumpy peg-like teeth, good for crushing the hard carapaces of insects. *Batrachognathus* is assumed to have been able to catch the abundant insects over the lake while in flight, like modern swallows and swifts do. A wide mouth like this would have been an ideal adaptation for the scooping action required. *Batrachognathus* was actually found back in 1948 but it is only since the renewed world interest in pterosaurs in the 1980s that it has become widely known.

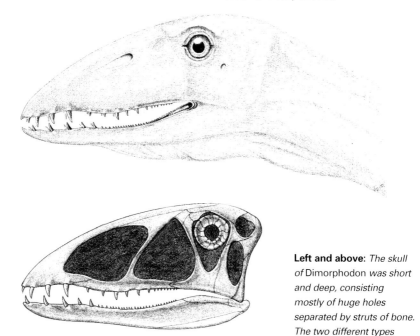

**Left and above:** *The skull of* Dimorphodon *was short and deep, consisting mostly of huge holes separated by struts of bone. The two different types of teeth give the animal its name.*

**Left and above:** *We do not know how rhamph-orhynchoids behaved on the ground. Possibly they ran on their hind legs, with their wings tucked away. The tail was a stiff rod, solidified by bony tendons that lashed the vertebrae together.*

# Advanced Rhamphorhynchoids

In early Jurassic times the great Tethys Ocean overflowed its banks and spread as a shallow sea across the continent of Europe. Most of Scandinavia and parts of northern Britain and Spain were dry land, but most of the rest of Europe was under a warm shallow sea with dotted islands. This is reflected in the thick deposits of marine

*The rhamphorhynchoids, such as Dorygnathus (left) and Campylognathoides (right), may have spent their time fishing along the shores of the Jurassic continents.*

limestones and shales found in many places dating from this time. One famous occurrence is in Württemberg, in southern Germany, where thin slabs of limestone have been mined for building and decoration for centuries. This area is famous for its fossils of marine reptiles. The best of the world's ichthyosaur fossils are found there. The preservation is so good that the body shape can be seen outlined in a silhouette of carbon on the rocks. Fossils like this show the arrangement of fins that would not normally be fossilized, leading to an early appreciation of what the ichthyosaurs looked like and showing how similar they were to sharks and dolphins. There were also remains of long-necked plesiosaurs, sea crocodiles, fish, and all sorts of invertebrates such as ammonites, sea lilies, and bivalves. There are also pterosaurs.

## HISTORICAL PTEROSAUR SITE

The first pterosaur finds were made in 1856, in the quarries around Holzmaden. The area is now internationally regarded as so important that the quarries were declared a protected area in 1979. Two important pterosaurs are known from this area. As it is early in the history of pterosaurs, they are both rhamphorhynchoids.

*Dorygnathus* had a bunch of curving fangs at the front of the jaws that intermeshed when the jaws were closed. These appear to be adaptations for catching fish, like most of its

*The fine-grained lagoon deposits in Germany have yielded many late Jurassic pterosaurs, some of them tiny including snaggle-toothed* Scaphognathus *(left), and broad-faced* Anurognathus *(right), which, despite being a rhamphorhynchoid, had a short tail.*

relatives. It was about the size of a crow, with short wings, probably for agile maneuvering. The legs, like the legs of *Dimorphodon*, were quite long and powerful. Also like *Dimorphodon* the feet had four strong claws, and the fifth toe stuck out at a strange angle. This is only guesswork, but it is possible that this toe supported a web of skin that was used in steering while in flight, or to act like the webbed foot of a duck—to move the animal about when it was sitting on the water and to help to get it airborne from the sea surface.

Much larger, about the size of a buzzard, was the other main pterosaur from that area, *Campylognathoides*. It differs from *Dorygnathus* in having a shorter head and smaller teeth. The tips of its jaws come to an upward-curving point. It does not have the distinctive fifth toe; its fifth toe is much smaller.

## CAUGHT IN TIME

The lower Jurassic deposits of Holzmaden are spectacular. However, they are nothing compared with the upper Jurassic deposits of Solnhofen. The thinly bedded limestone here was

laid down in shallow lagoons, cut off by reefs from the deeper ocean to the south. The chemistry of these lagoons was toxic, and anything swimming in from more healthy areas died quickly and was preserved as a fossil. Fossils of fish are found here, as are fossils of ammonites that have left impressions on the substrate where they hit the bottom and fell over, and horseshoe crabs lying dead at the end of their trail of footprints. The islands of the lagoons and the surrounding lands were arid, and so there was no terrestrial sediment washed in. The fauna of these islands preserved in the limestones include the perfect remains of dinosaurs, like *Compsognathus*, lizards, the early bird *Archaeopteryx*, and many pterosaurs.

One of these was *Scaphognathus*. It

230    220    210    200    190    180    170    160    15

TRIASSIC                          JURASSIC

DORYGNATHUS

COMPSOGNATHUS

RHAMPHORHYNCHUS

**Left and right:** *We know most about the rhamphorhynchoids from the remains of* Rhamphorhynchus *itself. It is one of the pterosaurs found in the fine-grained lagoon deposits of Germany, and so we know not only its skeleton but details of its wing membrane as well. There were at least five different species of* Rhamphorhynchus, *differing from one another mostly by size, as shown by these skulls.*

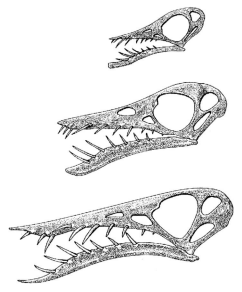

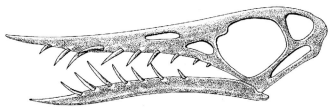

| 140 | 130 | 120 | 110 | 100 | 90 | 80 | 70 | 60 |
|-----|-----|-----|-----|-----|-----|-----|-----|-----|

CRETACEOUS

SCATHOGNATHUS

ANUROGNATHUS

DENDRORHYNCHOIDES

COMODACTYLUS

was rather snaggle-toothed, with only a few big teeth—eighteen in the upper jaw and ten in the lower—separated by big gaps. Probably another adaptation to fish eating.

One of the strangest pterosaurs of all, was found here. It was tiny, only sparrow sized, and is called *Anurognathus*. Its head was short and rounded, and it had peg-like teeth. Like *Batrachognathus* from Kazakhstan, it was probably an insect-eater, catching flying insects from the air. The wings were long and narrow, like those of a swallow, backing up this idea. The tail is strange for a rhamphorhynchoid. It is short and stumpy, a feature that is usually found on a pterodactyloids. However the shape of the hands and other features show that it is actually a specialized rhamphorhynchoid.

## THE TWO FAMILIES

The difference between the rhamph-orhynchoids and the pterodactyloids is quite evident at Solnhofen. In these deposits we find the remains of both groups. Here we find *Rhamphorhynchus* itself, as well as *Pterodactylus*.

*Rhamophorhynchus* is present in about half a dozen different species, ranging in size from the wingspan of a sparrow to the wingspan of a seagull. The largest seems to form two distinct groups based on the length of a skull and the length of the wing finger. This is taken as an indication of two different sexes, although we cannot tell which is which. They all have pointed jaws and teeth that are thrust forward. Apart from this they all have the same body plan of the other rhamphorhynchoids already described.

*Rhamphorhynchus* represent one of the last of the rhamphorhynchoids. Fossils of possible other species of *Rhamphorhynchus* are known from Portugal, from England, and from East Africa—another find from an early twentieth century German expedition. A similar form, *Comodactylus*, comes from the contemporary Morrison Formation of North America. Rhamphorhynchoids are found in some early Cretaceous rocks, such as *Dendrorhynchoides* from the famous lake deposits in Liaoning Province—the site of the famous Chinese half-bird-half-dinosaur beasts—but the late Jurassic Solnhofen lagoons mark the end of their heyday. From then onward their relatives, the pterodactyloids, were the main pterosaur group.

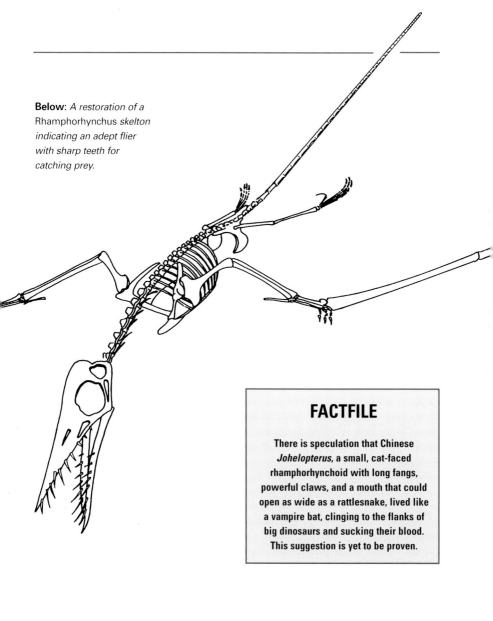

**Below:** *A restoration of a* Rhamphorhynchus *skelton indicating an adept flier with sharp teeth for catching prey.*

## FACTFILE

There is speculation that Chinese *Johelopterus*, a small, cat-faced rhamphorhynchoid with long fangs, powerful claws, and a mouth that could open as wide as a rattlesnake, lived like a vampire bat, clinging to the flanks of big dinosaurs and sucking their blood. This suggestion is yet to be proven.

# Primitive Pterodactyloids

The differences between the rhamphorhynchoids and the pterodactyloids can be tabulated. Rhamphorhynchoids had long tails; pterodactyloids had short tails. Rhamphorhynchoids had short wrist bones; pterodactyloids had long wrist bones, taking the free fingers of the hand further down the wing. Rhamphorhynchoids had short necks; pterodactyloids had long necks. Rhamphorhynchoids held their heads forward parallel to the neck; pterodactyloids held their heads at an angle, like those of birds. Rhamphorhynchoids had long fifth toes, possibly something to do with the attachment of membranes; pterodactyloids had short fifth toes, sometimes absent altogether. All these features are seen side by side in the limestones of Solnhofen.

## WING DETAILS

The pterosaurs, both rhamphorhynchoids and pterodactyloids, are so well preserved that we can actually see the membrane of the wings. Once it was thought that the wing membrane of a pterosaur was a simple sheet of skin, flexible but delicate and vulnerable. Detailed fossils now show that it was actually quite a complex structure. It was reinforced by bunches of keratin fibers that projected backwards

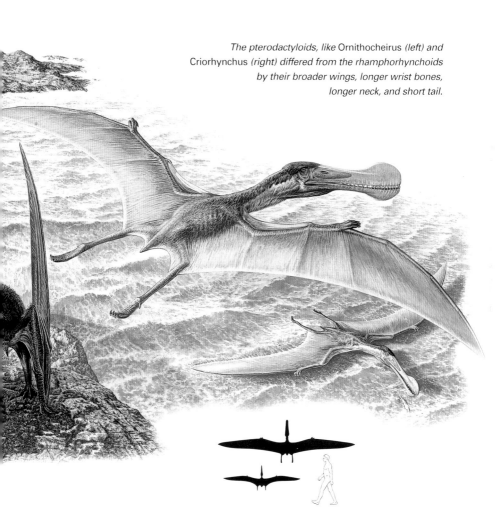

The pterodactyloids, like Ornithocheirus *(left) and*
Criorhynchus *(right) differed from the rhamphorhynchoids*
*by their broader wings, longer wrist bones,*
*longer neck, and short tail.*

from the arms, and radiated away from the hand. The pattern formed is very similar to the way that the flight feathers are arranged on the wing of a bird. Evidently it is a pattern that lends itself to withstanding all the stresses that will be called upon the wing while in flight.

What is still to be discovered, though, is just how that wing was attached to the body and particularly to the hind legs and the tail. Perhaps it was attached to the entire length of the leg, right down to the ankles. Perhaps it was attached only to the thigh. Perhaps it was not attached to the leg at all and just ended at the waist. And was it attached to the tail? Perhaps there was another membrane in the space between the legs and the tail. Perhaps this space was kept clear. Perhaps, as seem to be suggested by the remains of *Sordes*, a membrane went directly between the legs missing out the tail altogether. For all the detail of the Solnhofen specimens, these are matters that have still to be settled.

## FLYING ACTION

In the distant past, it was assumed that the pterosaurs could do little in the way of powered flight. Because they existed before birds, it was believed that they

were more primitive than birds, and had not evolved a bird's flying ability. In the minds of early paleontologists the pterosaurs merely glided about on outstretched wings without any muscular action at all. We now

understand that the pterosaurs were very strong fliers, and had some quite sophisticated flying techniques.

On the front of a pterosaur's long wrist bones, there was a small bone that curved back toward the shoulder.

This was once interpreted as the atrophied remains of a finger, but is now thought to have been an extension of one of the hand bones. It seems likely that this supported a smaller flight membrane in front of the arm. Birds have an important little feather, the alula, in exactly the same position. They use this to alter the flow of air over the wing, and so control the speed and attitude of flight. The front arm membrane of the pterosaur must have been used for exactly the same purpose.

## CRESTED FISHERS

*Pterodactylus* was the archetypal pterodactyl, but there were many more, dating from the late Jurassic to the end of the Cretaceous. *Criorhynchus* was a big sea-going form from the Cretaceous. Like all pterodactyloids it had the long arms and wrist bones, the short legs and the big head. Its oddest feature was the front of the skull. The snout was not pointed but blunt and solid. On the top it had a semicircular crest. We do not know of the front of the lower jaw, but comparing the animal with other closely related pterodactyloids we can assume that

**Above:** *Many of the primitive pterodactyloids, such as* Ceradactylus *(left),* Anhanguera *(middle), and* Tropeognathus *(top), showed all sorts of adaptations, with specialist teeth or head crests, for fishing.*

there was a corresponding semicircular crest on the lower jaw as well. The small sharp teeth were a fish-eater's teeth. It seems likely that this crest was used in fishing. When the flying animal dipped its snout into the water the crest would have acted as a kind of aquafoil, and kept the snout steady. A few other pterosaurs had similar structures.

*Ornithocheirus* was more conventional looking. It was one of the most abundant pterosaurs of the Cretaceous and was found worldwide.

*Anhanguera* and *Tropeognathus* were other fish-eating pterodactyloids that had the crests on the snout and the lower jaw. These were found in Brazil and were much better preserved than *Criorhynchus*. They were not discovered until the 1980s, but their study shed new light on the appearance and lifestyle of *Criorhynchus*, which scientists had been puzzling over since its discovery and study by Sir Richard Owen in the 1870s. These were all very big animals, approaching the size of an albatross in wingspan.

## AMERICAN FORMS

Across North America in late Cretaceous times there stretched a seaway, called the Niobrara Sea. This

**Right:** *Some of the late Cretaceous pterodactyloids were toothless. This, however, does not seem to have detracted from their ability to fish. Two* Nyctosaurus *(center) and two species of* Pteranodon *fished the continental seaway of North America.*

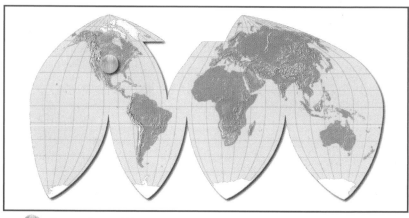

Pteranodon and Nyctosaurus

ran north to south, separating the region of the Rocky Mountains from that of the Appalachians and the east coast. The remains of all sorts of pterosaurs have been found in the chalk and shale that were laid down in this sea. Perhaps the most famous of these was *Pteranodon*.

Until recently *Pteranodon* was regarded as the biggest pterosaur of all. In fact, with a wingspan of some 30 feet (9 meters) it was suspected that it would have been impossible for anything larger to have been able to fly at all. This assumption has proved erroneous, but we shall come to that.

| 230 | 220 | 210 | 200 | 190 | 180 | 170 | 160 | 15 |
|---|---|---|---|---|---|---|---|---|

TRIASSIC
JURASSIC
PTERODACTYLL

*Pteranodon* had a huge head with a crest that jutted upward and backward. Several species of *Pteranodon* are known, and they had different-shaped crests. The crests could have had some aerodynamic function, but may have only been there for display. The feature of *Pteranodon* that we have not seen in earlier pterosaurs was the complete lack of teeth. Perhaps Pteranodon scooped its fish prey from the surface of the Nirobrara Sea and held it in a pelican-like pouch until it returned to land and could digest it, or feed it to its youngsters.

In the same upper Cretaceous sediments we find *Nyctosaurus*. This was very similar to *Pteranodon* in appearance, but it was much smaller and only had a small crest.

## ON THE GROUND

What a pterosaur actually looked like while it was on the ground, is an ongoing debate among paleontologists. It could be that it sprawled out like a lizard and could not be very active. In which case it would have spent much of its non-flying time clinging to cliff faces or tree trunks. They may even have hung upside down like bats. An alternative hypothesis has them walking like quadrupedal dinosaurs, with their limbs held below them. Other scientists will have them walking on hind legs like birds, with their wings

### FACTFILE

In 1831 August Goldfuss suggested that pterosaurs were warm-blooded animals and must have been covered in fur, like bats. Over the next century several scientists suggested the same thing. It was only with the discovery of *Sordes* with its unmistakeable impression of hair that the idea became widely accepted.

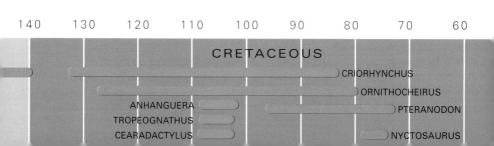

CRETACEOUS

CRIORHYNCHUS
ORNITHOCHEIRUS
ANHANGUERA
PTERANODON
TROPEOGNATHUS
CEARADACTYLUS
NYCTOSAURUS

tucked neatly to their sides and held clear of the ground. There is not much evidence for any of these theories.

Footprints do give us some clues. There are many sets of footprints around the world that are purported to have been made by pterosaurs. These show sets of four-toed footprints—the hind feet—and, wider apart, sets of three-toed marks with a kind of a swirl curling away from them—the hands and the finger carrying the wing. This would suggest the four-footed stance for a grounded pterosaur, with a gait somewhat similar to someone walking on crutches.

**Above and right:** *There is little agreement amongst scientists on how pterodactyloids behaved on the ground. Some think they walked on all fours (as seen above), but other think they were bipedal like birds (as seen below).*

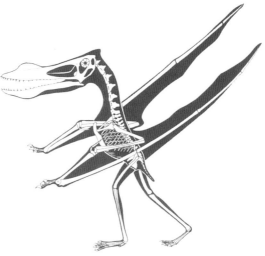

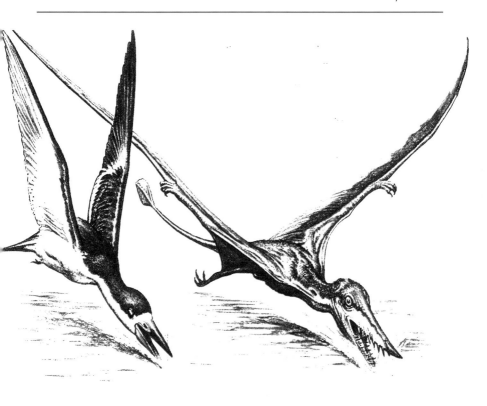

**Above:** *Some pterosaurs such as* Rhamphorynchus *may have used fishing techniques similar to those practised by the black skimmer, which ploughs its lower jaw through the surface of the water during flight.*

# Advanced Pterodactyloids

The body shape of the pterodactyloid (meaning "winged finger") was quite conservative, however, there were several variations on the shape of the head.

*Germanodactylus*, found in topmost Jurassic rocks of Germany, had long narrow jaws and a toothless beak at the front. It also had a crest that ran from above the eyes, down past the nostrils, to well down its snout. It was probably covered in a horny sheath and would have been brightly colored.

If *Germanodactylus* was a pterosaur from Germany, then *Gallodactylus*, from its name, was a pterosaur from France. It also had a crest on the head, but this extended backward. The teeth were interesting, being concentrated at the front of the mouth. These must also have been fish-eaters, hunting along the northern shoreline and in the lagoons of the Tethys. So far it seems as if the pterosaurs were either big and fish eating,

*Medium-sized pterodactyloids existed all over the world.* Gallodactylus *(above) and* Germanodactylus *(right) were typical European examples.*

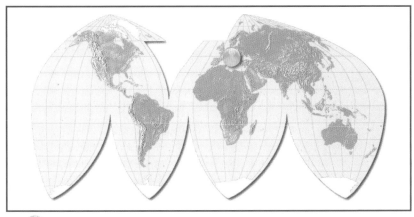

Gallodactylus and Germanodactylus

or small and insectivorous. There were, however, other pterosaur diets and these were reflected in the unique shapes of the mouth and teeth.

### FILTER-FEEDERS

*Ctenochasma* was an unusual pterodactyloid that lived among the various fish-eaters of the Solnhofen lagoons. It was found in 1851 and the name means "comb jaw"—a look at the fossil (see page 231) will show why. *Ctenochasma* had a low skull with long narrow jaws, curved slightly upward, and equipped with masses of long slender teeth. These teeth, there were over 250 of them, spread outward and curved upward, forming an ideal sieve. It would have stood in the shallow water swinging its jaws about on the surface, trapping plankton and floating organisms such as little crustaceans and insect larvae, very much like flamingos do today.

Another filter feeder of the Solnhofen deposits was *Gnathosaurus*. It is only known from two skull specimens. These are somewhat similar to the skull of *Ctenochasma*, but the teeth are a little coarser and arranged in a kind of a rosette at the front of the mouth. When it was first discovered back in 1832 it was assumed to have been the skull of some kind of a crocodile. There are modern crocodiles, gavials, which have long slender jaws and masses of fine teeth. These are used for catching fish, but it is not unreasonable to assume that this adaptation could be taken to an extreme, producing very lightweight jaws with dense rows of comb-like teeth as an adaptation to filter feeding.

A second skull of this animal was found in 1951, which was in better condition; showing it to have been a pterosaur. No other bones of this animal have been found so we must deduce that the rest of the body was similar to that of the other pterodactyloids.

The filter feeding adaptation was taken to an extreme by the Argentinean early Cretaceous form *Pterodaustro*. The skull is so highly adapted that it would be impossible to interpret it in any other way. The jaws are extremely long and curve upward. The lower jaw was equipped with a groove at each side in which were set masses and masses of tightly packed bristles. These may be adapted teeth, or they may

have evolved in some completely different way.

As in the Solnhofen examples it would have stood on all fours in the shallow water and scooped at the water surface with its lower jaw. The water would have strained out between the bristles leaving the plankton trapped in the mouth. The upper jaw was equipped with short blunt teeth that would have broken up anything big that had been caught in the plankton basket.

In the 1980s pterosaur experts put an intriguing suggestion forward. Flamingos gain their pink coloration from the chemicals absorbed from the crustaceans they eat. These produce the pink pigmentation in the keratin of their feathers. Perhaps, if *Pterodasustro* and the other filter-feeding pterosaurs had the same diet as flamingos, the same pigments would have been deposited in the keratin of their hairy coats. Perhaps these pterosaurs were pink also.

## THE POWER OF FLIGHT

In all flying animals—such as birds, bats, and pterosaurs—the motion is achieved by a flapping action. The wing muscles provide the power. The wings

*Some pterodactyloids were equipped as filter-feeding animals.* Ctenochasma *(bottom left)* and Gnathosaurus *(top) had very fine comb-like teeth for sifting small organisms from still water.*

are convex on the upper surface and concave on the lower. A forward motion of a surface with this geometry provides lift, with the passage of air over the upper surface producing a region of reduced pressure into which the wing will rise. Theoretically the greatest curve would have been closest to the body, with the wingtips having a much shallower profile. The motion of the flying animal is forward, to enable the wings to produce this lift. The anatomy of a pterosaur is geared to achieving this forward action.

In all pterosaurs the shoulder girdle is fused into a single bone. This give a firm base into which the arm articulates. In birds the flying muscles are firmly anchored to an expanded breastbone called the sternum. A similar broad breastbone existed in the pterosaurs, compact enough to prevent the rib cage from collapsing under the pressure of the action of the flight muscles.

The angle of the wing bones shows that on the downstroke the wing would have traveled to about twenty degrees below the horizontal plane, while in the upstroke it would have been carried to about sixty degrees

The most extreme form of filter-feeding pterodactyloid was Pterodaustro. *Its jaws were equipped with a brush-like array of fine fibers. It must have fed like a modern flamingo.*

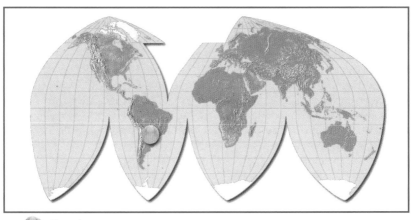

Pterodaustro

above it. The wing bone would have been able to rotate in the shoulder socket so that the downstroke would have driven the flying animal onward. This is just like the action of a bird's wing.

Complex flying action such as this takes a tremendous amount of brainpower just to coordinate it. Occasionally we find the cast of a pterosaur brain, formed when the empty skull filled with sediment and this infilling solidified to stone. Endocasts like this may not show the internal structure of the different parts of the brain but they certainly indicate

230      220      210      200      190      180      170      160      15

TRIASSIC                                          JURASSIC

the volume of the different sections, and a great deal can be inferred from these dimensions.

The best pterosaur endocast so far found was about the size of an almond and found in Jurassic rocks of northern England in the late nineteenth century. The brain was considerably larger than that of other reptiles of a similar size. The region of the brain dedicated to muscular coordination—that which would control maneuverability in flight and in takeoff and landing—was even bigger than we see in birds of comparable size.

The part of the brain dealing with smell was small, but the part dealing with vision appears to be well developed, indicating that it hunted by sight rather than by smell. On the whole the pterosaurs had brains that were bigger than those of other reptiles, although not as big as those of modern birds.

The wing bones were hollow—an adaptation for reducing the weight of the animal—just as in birds. Inside the hollows a network of bony struts gave strength to support the bones. The pattern was totally in keeping with the forces that would have acted on the bone—they were a solid reflection of the lines of force. Parts of the rest of the skeleton were made of spongy bone.

## FACTFILE

Sometimes the skull of a pterosaur is well enough preserved to give scientists an idea of the brain capacity. These show large optic lobes, suggesting very good eyesight—something that is also suggested by the big eye sockets. The size of a pterosaur's brain lies somewhere between that of a crocodile and that of a bird.

| 140 | 130 | 120 | 110 | 100 | 90 | 80 | 70 | 60 |
|-----|-----|-----|-----|-----|----|----|----|----|

CRETACEOUS

GERMANODACTYLUS
GALLODACTYLUS
CTENOCHASMA
GNATHOOSAURUS
PTERADAUSTRO

**Right and below:** *The most famous pterodactyloid is* Pterodactylus *itself. There were a number of species, each differing in the shape and size of the head, such as these shown here. The length of the skull varied from 1.65 inches (42 centimeters) to 4.25 inches (10.8 centimeters).*

**P. elegans**

**P. micronyx**

**P. kochi**

**P. antiquus**

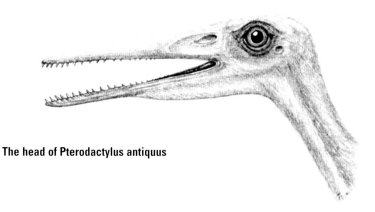

**The head of Pterodactylus antiquus**

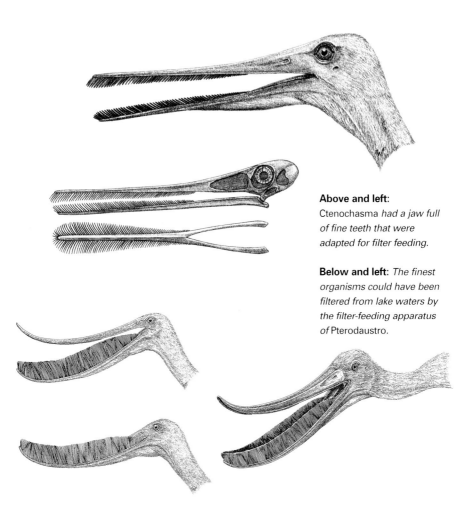

**Above and left:**
Ctenochasma *had a jaw full of fine teeth that were adapted for filter feeding.*

**Below and left:** *The finest organisms could have been filtered from lake waters by the filter-feeding apparatus of* Pterodaustro.

# Forceps-Jawed Relatives

Imagine an animal with a triangular head, deep and narrow at the back where the small eye sockets are, and narrowing to an upward-curving beak that comes to a point like a pair of forceps. Instead of teeth give it a row of bony knobs along the side of the jaws. Now give it a crest. This is *Dsungaripterus*.

Just what did this beast do with a set of jaws like this? The most likely answer is that it caught and ate shellfish, winkling them out with its forceps-like beak and crushing them with its bony knobs.

A smaller form, *Phobetor* turned up in 1982, but this had proper teeth instead of the bony knobs. Similar pterosaurs have been coming to light more recently and it looks as if there was a whole family of crested, forceps-billed shellfish-eaters in early Cretaceous Asia.

Nor was this group confined to Asia. *Domeykodactylus* is from Chile. This had a series of brush-like fibers sprouting from the crest—possibly from a soft tissue ornament that since rotted away.

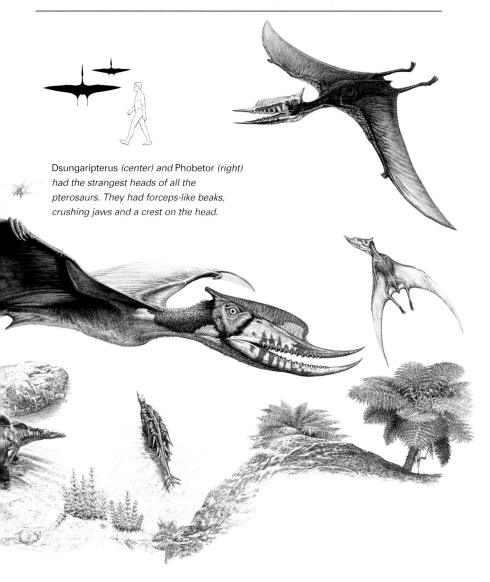

Dsungaripterus *(center)* and Phobetor *(right)* had the strangest heads of all the pterosaurs. They had forceps-like beaks, crushing jaws and a crest on the head.

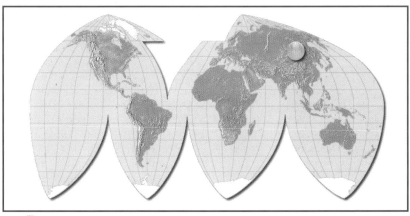

Dsungaripterus and Phobetor

## THE BIG CRESTS OF BRAZIL

If we wish to see even more spectacular crests on pterosaurs we must turn our attention to South America. A site in Brazil, called Araripe, which had been famous for fossil fish since 1817 threw up its first pterosaur skull in 1971. Several pterosaurs have since been discovered here in a remarkable state of preservation. The chemistry of the lake in which the sediments formed in early Cretaceous times began to alter the bones as soon as the animals died and fossilization took place very quickly. *Tapejara* had a short skull, with toothless jaws, and a

| 230 | 220 | 210 | 200 | 190 | 180 | 170 | 160 | 1 |

TRIASSIC                                    JURASSIC

crest that swept upward and back. This would have supported a kind of a sail that represented about five sixths of the area of the skull. The purpose of this is still a mystery. It would be no good for aerodynamics—it would just get in the way. It would have been of no help in gathering food—*Tapejara* was probably a fruit-eater and the crest would have been entangled in branches. It must have been a display structure.

Another absurdly huge pterosaur crest from this area belongs to *Tupuxuara*. The crest of this genus starts at the tip of the beak, rises above the upper jaw, and passes out behind the skull like an oar, doubling the length of the skull. It was hollow, made up from two slabs of bone less than a 0.04 inches (1 millimeter) thick. Something about the lake environments of South America must have led to the evolution of these unusual crests.

## FACTFILE

The wing bone of a pterosaur was extremely thin, maybe only about 0.02 inches (0.5mm) thick. The hollow inside the bone was strengthened by bony struts that were angled in the direction needed to withstand the forces involved in flying. This arrangement gave the greatest strength for the least weight.

**Above:** *The skull of* Phobetor *was similar to that of* Dsungaripterus, *but had teeth instead of the tubercles in the jaws.*

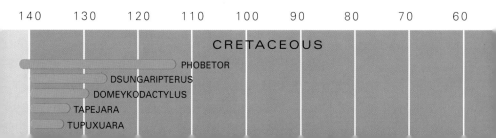

140    130    120    110    100    90    80    70    60

CRETACEOUS

PHOBETOR
DSUNGARIPTERUS
DOMEYKODACTYLUS
TAPEJARA
TUPUXUARA

# The Giants

Until the 1970s it was believed that *Pteranodon* was the biggest pterosaur of them all, and that it reached the limits of size achievable by a flying animal. That was before the discovery of *Quetzalcoatlus*. Named after the feathered serpent deity of the Aztecs, this creature was first thought to have had a wingspan of 51 feet (15.5 meters) when the wing bones came to light in the topmost Cretaceous beds of Texas. Subsequent bones allowed a fuller idea of this animal and the wingspan was reduced to 36–39 feet (12 meters). An animal the size of this must have weighed nearly 200 pounds (80–90 kilograms). The muscular power and control to fly a body this size must have been enormous. It seems that it was full of weight-saving devices, such as the lack of teeth in the jaws—a strategy used by the birds—and a skull that was made of honeycombed bone that must have had the consistency and lightness of expanded polystyrene.

It was an enormous animal, with rather short wings for the size of the body. The neck was long and stiff, allowing no side-to-side movement. The skull had long toothless jaws with sharp edges, probably covered in horn to give a kind of a beak like that of a bird.

The biggest pterosaurs, such as Quetzalcoatlus, were the size of small aircraft. They lived far inland, soaring on rising air thermals over the continent.

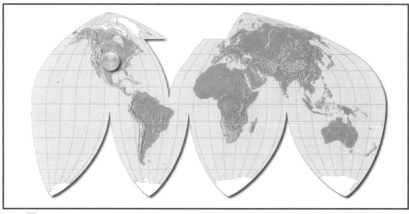

Quetzalcoatlus

## A FEAST OF GIANTS

Another big pterosaur is *Arambourgiana* from the upper Cretaceous of Jordan. It was first discovered back in the 1950s but it has only recently been studied properly. It is known from a single neck vertebra, which is almost 2 feet (60 centimeters) long. Its original, more evocative, name was *Titanopteryx* (meaning "giant wing") but this had already been given to something else—to an insect no less—and so it had to be changed. *Azhdarcho* is yet another, from Uzbekistan.

All of these pterosaurs have

230     220     210     200     190     180     170     160     15

TRIASSIC                                        JURASSIC

extremely long and stiff necks. There is still a great deal of uncertainty as to what they ate and how they lived. They were not seagoing beasts, as they have all been found in areas that were well inland during their time. It has been suggested that they probed in the mud of freshwater lakes for invertebrates. Another suggestion is that they soared in the skies above the late cretaceous plains like vultures, waiting for the telltale signs of a dying animal, and then circled in and waited for its death before feasting on its flesh and scavenging its organs.

## NESTING COLONIES?

There is no good evidence to tell us about the social or family life of pterosaurs—any pterosaurs. One interesting discovery, though, took place in the 1990s in Chile. In early Cretaceous rocks was a bed of sand and gravel about 6½ feet (2 meters) deep covering an area of about a half a square mile (1 square kilometer). It was a flood deposit, laid down by a sudden flash flood in the flat desert terrain that would have occupied the area at that time. In that deposit was the biggest collection of pterosaur bones ever discovered. They were all bones of youngsters of the same species, and the interpretation was that a nesting colony of fledglings incapable of flight

---

### FACTFILE

The extinction of the pterosaurs at the end of the Cretaceous period was not a sudden event. There was a noticeable decrease in their diversity in late Cretaceous times, only the few types of giants remaining at the very end. Widespread destruction caused by a meteorite impact would only have finished off a decline that was already under way.

---

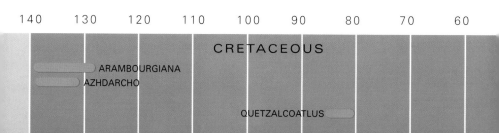

| 140 | 130 | 120 | 110 | 100 | 90 | 80 | 70 | 60 |

CRETACEOUS

ARAMBOURGIANA

AZHDARCHO

QUETZALCOATLUS

had been suddenly washed away and destroyed. So it looks as if at least one type of big pterosaur nested on the ground in colonies, in deserts, on flat land, a long way from the sea.

*Quetzalcoatlus* was not only one of the biggest of the pterosaurs, it was also one of the last to evolve. It existed right up until the end of the Cretaceous period when it, along with all of its dinosaurian contemporaries, became extinct. The skies were now clear to be dominated by a different group of flying animal—the dinosaurs' descendants, the birds.

A brief run down like this shows a

**Above and right:** *We do not really know how the monster pterosaurs like* Quetzalcoatlus *fed. It may have lived on carrion, or it may have fished for shellfish in inland lakes and rivers.*

dazzling array of types of pterosaur. Primitive long-tailed types, evolving into short-tailed efficient fliers with all the adaptations we would expect for a world-wide group of animals—small insect-eaters, snaggle-toothed fishers, comb-jawed plankton feeders, huge carrion-eaters. The range of types rivals the range of birds we see today.

To date we have identified between sixty and seventy different genera of pterosaur. They existed for about 155 million years—about the same length of time that birds have existed. There must have been many thousands of different types of pterosaur that we will never know about. The problem is that those we know come from river deposits or shallow sea deposits—the areas where things are most likely to fossilize. We know almost nothing of pterosaurs that lived far inland, in forests or in mountainous terrain, where lightweight bones that comprised the pterosaur skeleton would never have survived the onslaughts of carrion-eaters or the physical processes of erosion. Pterosaur specialist Peter Wellnhofer has estimated that we have identified less than one percent of the pterosaurs that ever existed.

As with the study of dinosaurs, one of the most intriguing aspects of studying these beasts is the knowledge that, however much we find out, whatever new discoveries come to light, we will never know everything. There will always be something more to find.

# Early Flying Animals

Although the pterosaurs were the most important flying animals of the age of reptiles, they were by no means the first.

An early flying device used by reptiles was the gliding wing supported on outgrowths of the ribs. This first appeared in the Permian with *Coelurosauravus*, from Germany and its relative *Deadalosaurus* from Madagascar. The wings were not very sophisticated and would not have allowed for powered flight, or much in the way of

**Below:** Icarosaurus *was a Permian gliding reptile, with a similar gliding mechanism to that of Coelurosauravus.*

**Right:** Longisquama *had an arrangement of long scales along its back. These may have been used as gliding wings.*

**Below:** Coelurosauravus, *from the Permian, was an early attempt at flight. It glided by wings stretched out on elongated ribs.*

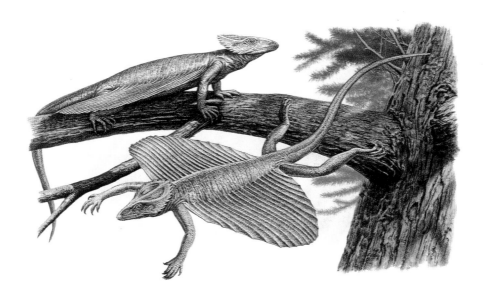

maneuverability. However, they seem to have worked. It was such a successful design that it reappeared in Triassic *Icarosaurus* and *Kuehneosaurus*. It even exists today, in the flying lizard *Draco* of Malaysia. If modern *Draco* is anything to go by, these earlier reptiles probably also used their wings and brightly colored signaling devices as a camouflage trick to break up the typical lizard shape against the tree trunks.

**Left**: *The first true bird was* Archaeopteryx. *It lived just at the time when the* rhamphorhynchoids *were being replaced by the* pterodactyloids. *However, its descendants outlived both types of pterosaur.*

form a continuous gliding surface. The reptile was only about 4–5 inches (10–12.5 centimeters) long. It seems unlikely that such a device would have been able to support anything larger.

Also from the late Triassic comes *Sharovipteryx*. It looked like a back-to-front pterosaur, with enormously elongated hind limbs. These probably supported a gliding membrane. It has been suggested that *Sharovipteryx* was close to the ancestral line of the pterosaurs.

These evolutionary experiments soon passed. It was time for the pterosaurs to take over.

## MODERN MASTERS OF THE SKIES

About half way through the Mesozoic, while the pterosaurs were at their peak, a completely new group of flying animals arrived—the birds.

The first was *Archaeopteryx*, evolved from the small meat-eating dinosaurs, and similar to them in many ways.

More sophisticated was the gliding mechanism of late Triassic *Longisquama*. This consisted of a double row of greatly elongated scales along the backbone. It seems likely that these could have been spread out to

Although it had the plumage of a modern bird, and the layout of flying feathers on the wings was identical to that of modern birds, the skeleton was very much like that of a dinosaur. Instead of a beak it had a jaw full of sharp little teeth. Instead of a stumpy tail with a fan of feathers it had a long reptilian tail with feathers along the side.

On the front of the wings it had three pairs of claws. If it had not been for the impressions of feathers on the fossil it would have been classified as a small theropod dinosaur.

*Archaeopteryx* shared the skies with the pterosaurs. Its remains have been found in the limestone beds of Solnhofen, along with those of long-tailed rhamphorhynchoids and pterodactyloids.

As the evolution of birds continued

**Below and right:** *The skeleton of* Archaeopteryx *is intermediate between that of a small theropod dinosaur, such as* Compsognathus, *and that of a modern bird like a chicken.*

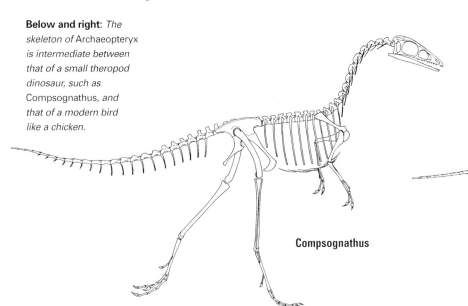

**Compsognathus**

the adaptations became more specialized. The development of a beak and short tail came soon after, as did the emplacement of the alula feather on the front of the wing.

By the time the pterosaurs and the whole panoply of dinosaurs—theropods, sauropods, ornithopods, armored, and horned dinosaurs, became extinct, the fully developed modern bird was ready to become what it is today—the most sophisticated flying creature ever evolved.

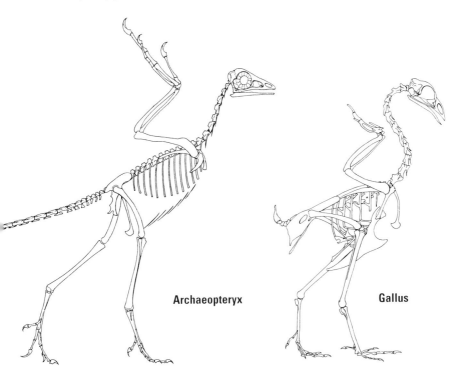

**Archaeopteryx**

**Gallus**

# Glossary

**Alula**
A controllable feather on the leading edge of the wing of a bird, at about the position of the thumb. It is used to regulate the flow of air over the wing. Sometimes called the "bastard wing."

**Ankylosaurid**
A member of the group of armored dinosaurs—those that had a club on the end of the tail.

**Aquafoil**
A blade that cuts through water, guiding itself by the angle it makes with the water passing around it.

**Aqualung**
A breathing aid consisting of a tank of air and a series of valves to allow a diver to breathe while underwater.

**Badlands**
Terrain, particularly in the western part of North America, consisting of gullies and pinnacles caused by erosion, so called because settlers found it "bad land" to cross.

**Ball-and-socket joint**
A joint consisting of a ball that fits inside a socket, allowing all-round freedom of movement between the two.

**Beak**
A mouthpart consisting of a ridge of horn.

**Binocular vision**
The ability to judge distance by focusing on a point with two eyes and being able to analyse the difference between the two images.

**Brachiosaurid**
A member of the long-necked plant-eating dinosaur group with the long front legs and tall shoulders.

**Camarasaurid**
A member of the long-necked plant-eating dinosaur group characterized by a square boxy skull and spoon-shaped teeth.

**Carnivore**
An animal that eats meat.

**Ceratopsian**
A member of the horned dinosaur group.

**Cold-blooded**
An animal that cannot regulate its body temperature by its own internal mechanisms.

**Crest**
A structure on top of the head, usually used for signaling or display.

**Cretaceous**
The last period of the Mesozoic era, lasting from 145 to 65 million years ago. This was the last period of the age of dinosaurs.

| | |
|---|---|
| **Derived** | Showing features that have developed from a more primitive ancestor. |
| **Diplodocid** | A member of the long-necked plant-eating dinosaur group, with a particularly long, low build. |
| **Display** | The act of communicating to another animal by means of visual signals. |
| **Endocast** | A cast formed by filling a hollow, such as the brain space in a skull, with some kind of material. |
| **Evolve** | To change, generation by generation, into new forms. |
| **Fang** | A sharp pointed tooth. |
| **Fermenting vat** | A container in which organic material is broken down by means of bacterial action. |
| **Fircula** | The wishbone of a bird. |
| **Fossilized** | Turned to stone through natural processes. |
| **Gait** | The way an animal walks. |
| **Genera** | The plural of genus—a classification that may cover several closely related species. |
| **Gizzard** | A region of the stomach containing pebbles or grit that can aid in digestion. |
| **Gondwana** | The southern part of the supercontinent of Pangaea. This eventually broke up to form the modern continents of South America, Africa, Inida, Australia and Antarctica. |
| **Herbaceous** | Growing close to the ground, without woody stems. |
| **Herbivore** | An animal that eats plants. |
| **Heterodontosaurid** | A member of the two-footed plant-eating dinosaur group with several types of teeth in the mouth—nipping teeth, stabbing teeth, and chewing teeth. |
| **Horn** | A hard structure formed from keratin. |
| **Ichnogenus** | The name given to an animal based only on its **footprint**. |
| **Ichthyosaur** | A member of a group of swimming reptiles, superficially resembling sharks or dolphins, that existed in the Mesozoic era |
| **Ilium** | The the hip bone that is attached to the backbone. |
| **Intestines** | The internal organs of an animal that deal with its digestion. |
| **Invertebrate** | An animal with no backbone. |
| **Ishium** | The hip bone that sweeps backwards from the hip socket. |
| **Jurassic** | The second period of the Mesozoic era, lasting from 208 to 145 million years ago. |

| | |
|---|---|
| **Keratin** | The organic chemical substance that forms hair, feathers, and horn. |
| **Limestone** | A sedimentary rock that has the mineral calcite as its principal component. |
| **Mesozoic** | The era of geological time stretching from 245 to 65 million years ago, consisting of the Triassic, Jurassic, and Cretaceous periods, and encompassing the age of the dinosaurs. |
| **Metabolism** | The physical and chemical processes involved in keeping an organism alive. |
| **Mollusc** | A shellfish, such as a clam or a snail. |
| **Nodosaurid** | A member of the group of armored dinosaurs—those that were distinguished by shoulder spines rather than by a club on the tail. |
| **Omnivorous** | Able to eat anything—meat or plants. |
| **Ontogeny** | The development of an individual. |
| **Ornithischian** | A dinosaur that had a bird-like arrangement of hip bones. |
| **Ornithopod** | The ornithischian group to which the two-footed plant-eaters belonged. The name means "bird-footed." |
| **Ossicles** | Small pieces of bone. |
| **Pachycephalosaurid** | A member of a group of dinosaurs, related to the ceratopsians, that had a thick bony roof to the head. |
| **Pangaea** | The supercontinent that existed at the beginning of the Mesozoic era, that comprised all the landmasses of the world. |
| **Pelvis** | The hip bones. |
| **Phytosaur** | A member of a group of crocodile-like animals that existed before the dinosaurs. |
| **Plesiosaur** | A member of a group of swimming reptiles, usually with long flexible necks, that existed in Mesozoic times. |
| **Preadaptation** | In evolution, the development of a pre-existing organ for some other purpose. |
| **Predentary** | In ornithischian dinosaurs, a bone in the front of the lower jaw. |
| **Primitive** | At an early stage in the evolutionary history of a group. |
| **Prosauropod** | A member of the earliest group of long-necked plant-eating dinosaurs |
| **Pubis** | The hip bone that points forward. |

| | |
|---|---|
| **Rhamphorhynchoid** | A member of the group of more primitive pterosaurs, characterized by a long tail and narrow wings. |
| **Saurischian** | A dinosaur that had a lizard-like arrangement of hip bones. |
| **Sauropod** | The saurischian group to which the long-necked plant-eaters belonged. The name means "lizard-footed." |
| **Scavenger** | An animal that eats meat that has been killed by something else, without actually huntingit. |
| **Scute** | Bony pieces embedded in the skin. |
| **Serrated** | Jagged and saw-like. |
| **Snorkel** | A tube that allows a diver to breathe underwater. |
| **Stegosaurid** | A member of the plated dinosaur group |
| **Taxonomist** | A scientist who studies the classification of living things. |
| **Tendon** | A strip of gristle connecting a muscle to a bone or one bone to another. |
| **Tendaguru fauna** | The collection of fossil animals including dinosaurs, very similar to those of late Jurassic North America, found at Tendaguru in what is now Tanzania by German expeditions early in the 120th century. |
| **Tethys** | The ocean that once separated Gondwana from the rest of the supercontinent of Pangaea. |
| **Thecodont** | The group of reptiles from which the dinosaurs and the pterosaurs evolved. They were characterized by the fact that their teeth grew in individual sockets. |
| **Theropod** | The saurischian group to which all the meat-eating dinosaurs belonged. The name means "beast-footed." |
| **Thyreophoran** | A member of the armored dinosaur or the plated dinosaur groups. |
| **Titanosaurid** | A member of the long-necked plant-eating dinosaur group, evolving late in their history and mostly having armor on the back |
| **Triassic** | The first part of the Mesozoic era, lasting from 245 to 208 million years ago. The dinosaurs evolved towards the end of the Triassic. |
| **Troodont** | A member of a group of light-weight meat-eating dinosaurs, that had high intelligence for a dinosaur. |
| **Warm-blooded** | Having an internal mechanism that regulates the body temperature. Mammals and birds are warm-blooded, as some of the dinosaurs may have been. |

# Index

# Picture Acknowledgements

All color and B&W illustrations of pterosaurs: © Peter Wellnhofer.

All color illustrations of dinosaurs: © Chrysalis Image Library/John Sibbick.

B&W illustrations of dinosaurs

| | | |
|---|---|---|
| R. Barsbold | C.W. Gilmore | F. Nopcsa |
| M. Borsuk-Bialynicka | W.L Holland | H.F. Osborn |
| B. Brown | J. Horner | J.H. Ostrom |
| C. Camp | W. Janensch | A.S. Romer |
| K. Carpenter | S.M. Kurzanov | D. Russell |
| A.J. Charig | L. Lambe | A.P. Santa-Luca |
| A.W. Crompton | R.S. Lull | E.M. Schlajiker |
| W.P. Coobs | A. Maleev | J.Sibbick |
| P. Dodson | O.C. Marsh | S.P. Welles |
| Dong Zhiming | B.H. Newman | R. Wild |